128 HWB

DAG HAMMARSKJÖLD'S WHITE BOOK

An Analysis of *Markings*

BY GUSTAF AULÉN

LONDON
S·P·C·K
1970

First published in the U.S.A. by Fortress Press, 1969
First published in Great Britain in 1970
by S.P.C.K.
Holy Trinity Church
Marylebone Road
London N.W.1

Printed offset in Great Britain by
The Camelot Press Ltd., London and Southampton

© Fortress Press, 1969

Grateful acknowledgment is made to Alfred A. Knopf, Inc., New York, and to Faber and Faber, Ltd., London, for permission to reprint from *Markings* by Dag Hammarskjöld, translated from the Swedish by Leif Sjöberg and W. H. Auden. Copyright © 1964 by Alfred A. Knopf, Inc. and Faber and Faber, Ltd.

SBN 281 02456 1

CONTENTS

Foreword	vii
Chapter 1. The Scope of *Markings*	1
The Publication of the Book	1
The Language of the Book	3
Two Retrospections	5
Chapter 2. Years of Crisis	9
Answering Yes without Knowing When	9
Tormenting Questions	13
A Growing Yes	22
Intellectual Difficulties	28
Chapter 3. Help on the Way	32
Albert Schweitzer	32
The Medieval Mystics	37
Meditations before the Gospels' Picture of Jesus	50
Chapter 4. Yes to God	58
Two Definitions of Faith	58
The Image of God	69
God and Christ	78
Destiny and the Meaning of Life	89
Chapter 5. The Way of Service	96
Service to God—Service to Men	96
"Dedicated"	104
Chapter 6. Retrospective Survey	113
Was Hammarskjöld a Mystic?	113
Some Comparisons: Luther, Kierkegaard, and Bonhoeffer	124
The Profile of Hammarskjöld's Faith	138

FOREWORD

In his letter to Leif Belfrage, printed as an Introduction to *Markings,* Dag Hammarskjöld described his diary as "a sort of *white book* concerning my negotiations with myself—and with God." *White book* and *negotiations* are expressions borrowed from the discourse of diplomacy. It is surely obvious that political affairs of the largest possible magnitude filled the later part of Hammarskjöld's life, and the reader of his diary must not be unaware of this background. It is, indeed, the very fact of this background which makes the diary unique among the *confessiones* of Christian history.

The white book itself, however, does not deal with political questions. It is from beginning to end concerned with its author's spiritual life. It is only natural, therefore, that during my studies of *Markings* I have often been reminded of the first great spiritual biography of the Christian era, *The Confessions of Saint Augustine.* There are parallels between the two books: a comparable relation between the author and his mother; the skepticism and struggle which marked the journey to faith. At the same time, however, we must not drive the similarities too far: *Markings* is wholly a work of our own time, a time radically different from that of Augustine of Hippo.

The purpose of the present study, then, is to give a thorough analysis of Dag Hammarskjöld's faith as it develops and is disclosed in *Markings:* an analysis—nothing more and nothing less, as strict as possible—of the contents of that remarkable book. We want to see what Hammarskjöld actually said about his faith, and what his sayings actually mean.

The diary has, on the whole, an aphoristic character. This is by no means surprising, especially when one recalls that during his years as Secretary General of the United Nations Hammarskjöld's entries in the diary must often have been written in haste, late at night, and after long

FOREWORD

hours of work. Nevertheless, the more I have worked with *Markings* the more I have been impressed by the consistency and coherence of Hammarskjöld's thought. At the end of my analysis, therefore, I have tried to show that his faith had a profile of its own. In this connection it is important to emphasize that in this book I have not the slightest desire to measure Hammarskjöld's faith by any particular standard or force him into any particular confessional mold. He must be allowed to speak for himself; he is surely worth listening to.

The important book of my friend Henry Pitney Van Dusen, *Dag Hammarskjöld: The Statesman and His Faith* (New York: Harper, 1967), provides a broad view of Hammarskjöld's life and career, and a general introduction to *Markings*. The character of my work is very different. Here I propose to concentrate exclusively and stringently upon an analysis of the *faith* of the "white book." This provides an opportunity for a detailed investigation of the intellectual, theological, and in some cases historical background for Hammarskjöld's views. In this connection my intimate knowledge of his Swedish background has been of considerable value.

The fact that the present study is based primarily on *Vägmärken* (Stockholm: Bonniers, 1963), the Swedish original of *Markings,* is not unimportant. Although all of my quotations are from the English book, it has still been necessary for me to indicate a rather large number of errors, some crucial, in that translation. Some of these errors might easily lead to misunderstandings; they have been caused most often by an imprecise use of technical religious and theological terminology, or by lack of familiarity with the idioms of the Swedish religious tradition. Entries from *Markings* which have been corrected have been indicated in this text by an asterisk (*).

Dag Hammarskjöld's White Book was written in English, and I wish to conclude my Foreword by expressing hearty thanks to my friend, Norman A. Hjelm. He has given excellent assistance in the revision of my English.

Gustaf Aulén

Lund, Sweden
March 1969

Chapter One

THE SCOPE OF MARKINGS

The Publication of the Book

Dag Hammarskjöld has already taken his place in universal world history. Much has been written concerning his work as Secretary General of the United Nations, and much more will be written in the future. At one point in *Markings* he speaks of the United Nations as "a feeble creation of men's hands—but," he continues, "you have to give your all to this human dream for the sake of that which alone gives it reality" (p. 100). No one can deny that Hammarskjöld did give his utmost in this tremendous engagement. His sense of duty and responsibility could hardly be surpassed, nor could the courage which he demonstrated in the most difficult and frightful situations. In an exposed position, and with a gigantic capacity for work, he toiled with stubborn tenacity for eight and a half years as Secretary General, becoming by degrees, we could say, an incarnation of the United Nations.

In *Markings* Hammarskjöld does not tell us anything about his actions as Secretary General, although many of the entries refer to different situations and events connected with the United Nations. In his distinguished volume, *Dag Hammarskjöld: The Statesman and His Faith*,[1] Henry Pitney Van Dusen has successfully undertaken an investigation of the political circumstances behind a number of the markings, and this research has in many cases aided our understanding of the entries in question. The fact remains, however, that the scope of *Markings* is not to discuss or elucidate political questions. Hammarskjöld rightly described his annotations as "a sort of *white book* concerning my negotiations with myself—and with God" (p. 7). In *Markings* he frankly discloses the

[1] Henry Pitney Van Dusen, *Dag Hammarskjöld: The Statesman and His Faith* (New York: Harper, 1967).

struggles of his inner life; he confesses his faith in God, and explains the meaning of this faith for, and the nature of its demands on, his life of action. *Markings* deals, from beginning to end, with the problems of Hammarskjöld's spiritual life.

The book has achieved a wide distribution. Van Dusen tells us that within a year and a half of the appearance of the English translation in 1964 the circulation of the book in the United States was no fewer than 450,000 copies, and that edition received its twenty-second printing in 1968. It has been translated into at least eleven languages.

Upon its publication, *Markings* encountered widely divergent reactions. However, at *one* point the reviewers were unanimous: the book was a general surprise. No one seems to have imagined that this man, sorely overworked as he was, could secretly have committed such annotations about his inner life to paper. In fact, the religious attitude demonstrated in *Markings* was itself a surprise for most people. *That* ought not to have been a surprise, however, for Hammarskjöld had not concealed his position. In a 1953 radio talk in America, arranged by Edward R. Murrow, he had openly confessed that he could endorse his Christian belief "without any compromise with the demands of the intellectual honesty which is the very key to maturity of mind." The following year this radio talk was published under the title "Old Creeds in a New World" (in the volume *This I Believe*, vol. 2).[2] On other occasions also Hammarskjöld had demonstrated a positive attitude towards Christian faith. Thus, readers ought to have been prepared to find religious questions dealt with in *Markings*. Nevertheless, it is easy to understand the general surprise. That surprise was traceable not only to the fact that the author held the world's most difficult civil office, but also to the exceptional character of the book itself. It is one thing on occasion to make statements such as Hammarskjöld had made, and it is quite a different matter year after year to write such confessions as we find in *Markings*. It is indeed appropriate here to recall the title of Augustine's famous work, *Confessiones*. There is no lack of memoirs in which authors tell us more or less about their spiritual experiences. But Hammarskjöld's "negotiations" do not belong to this category. Confessions of this type have few counterparts in Christian

---

[2] Dag Hammarskjöld, "Old Creeds in a New World," now found in *Servant of Peace*, ed. Wilder Foote (New York: Harper, 1962), pp. 23–24.

history. From one point of view his book is even unique, for such confessions are usually written by men or women who have lived quiet lives of meditation, while *Markings*—at least its larger part—was written by a statesman who bore all the troubles of the world.

The Language of the Book

When *Markings* first appeared it aroused certain formidable misunderstandings, especially on the part of some reviewers in Scandinavia. Hammarskjöld was accused of a self-exaltation which bordered on blasphemy. A review in one Stockholm journal was entitled "Did He See Himself as a Messiah?" The reviewer thinks that many statements in *Markings* indicate that the answer to his question ought to be "Yes." In another Stockholm journal a prominent critic wrote, "I believe it was a happy thing that Hammarskjöld died before his Christ dream had quite removed him from reality." And in a Danish journal diplomat Eyvind Bartels wrote that he considered *Markings* an attempt to create a "Hammarskjöld-myth in which the Secretary General appeared as a new Messiah."[3] According to Bartels this blasphemy was openly demonstrated. Interestingly enough, the Swedish criticisms were written from a position negative to Christian faith, but the Danish reviewer seems to have written more or less as a disciple of Kierkegaard. He examines Hammarskjöld's Christian faith and finds it very defective. A comparison of Kierkegaard and Hammarskjöld leads him to the following conclusion: They had some spiritual affinity, but they were different in that Kierkegaard had a deep and authentic Christian faith, and "behind his many dancing steps" he had a human heart such as we seek in vain in Hammarskjöld.

Accusations of this kind belong, as has already been said, to the time of the appearance of *Markings*. Since then they have ceased, and it is not to be expected that they will be repeated. It is only too obvious that the accusations are unfounded and quite unjustifiable. There is no reason to discuss them here, for my whole analysis of *Markings* will show how vast is the distance between the accusations and Hammarskjöld's own words.

[3] *Dag Hammarskjöld og hans Gud: En diskussion mellem Eyvind Bartels, Olov Hartman og Sven Stolpe* (Copenhagen: Kristeligt Dagblads Forlag, 1964), p. 21.

The relevant question is not whether Hammarskjöld considered himself a new Messiah; obviously he did not. Rather, we must ask how such absurd interpretations could be made. I shall not discuss this problem in detail since there are apparently different factors behind the Swedish and the Danish criticisms. However, two things ought to be emphasized. First, the critics isolate some statements from their contexts and fail to consider the testimony given by the pattern of *Markings* as a whole. And second, they fail to understand the religious language used by Hammarskjöld when, like the medieval mystics, he talks about his relation to Christ as *imitatio*—in the sense of "following Christ on his way of sacrifice." *Imitatio* here, as in the Bible, indicates not identity but discipleship. Hammarskjöld, it is clear, never considered himself as other than a disciple. Thus, any interpretation of *Markings* must rigorously observe and follow up the continuity which the book manifests in its own characteristic way, and also precisely understand the religious language used by Hammarskjöld, which is derived from biblical and other sources.

Now some general observations about the language of *Markings* are called for. In one of the entries (p.101) the theme is respect for the word. What Hammarskjöld says here may very well have reference to happenings in the United Nations; at the same time it is very characteristic of his attitude to language. *"Respect for the word* is the first commandment in the discipline by which a man can be educated to maturity—intellectual, emotional, and moral. Respect for the word—to employ it with scrupulous care and an incorruptible heartfelt love of truth—is essential if there is to be any growth in a society or in the human race. To misuse the word is to show contempt for man. It undermines the bridges and poisons the wells. It causes Man to regress down the long path of his evolution. 'But I say unto you, that every idle word that men speak' . . ." (p. 101). We remember the words hidden behind the ellipses: "they shall give account thereof in the day of judgment" (Matt. 12:36).

Respect for the word was for Hammarskjöld truly a commandment of principal importance. One can hardly read *Markings* without forming the impression that Hammarskjöld treats language with utmost care. Writing about his spiritual life and its problems, he has tried to find the right words, as precisely suited as possible for saying what he wants to say, what he himself acknowledges as truth. In light of the fact that he, in his self-examination, frankly and ruthlessly unmasks all that he considers defective, Bartel's idea about a freely built up Hammarskjöld-myth seems ridiculous.

The markings are often written with artistic mastery. Not only was Hammarskjöld a prominent connoisseur of literature and the arts, but he also devoted himself to his own literary creation—not least as translator of much modern poetry into Swedish. He became a member of the Swedish Academy, instituted for literature in 1786 by King Gustaf III, and this membership was completely justified. In *Markings* we find much poetry, not only in verse form but often also in entries written in prose.

What has been said here about the language of *Markings* does not mean that the book is always easy to understand. That is not the case. Hammarskjöld's style can be very clear, but not a few of the markings are difficult to grasp, and I do not pretend to be able myself to understand every word in the book. The difficulties confronting the interpreter have a variety of causes. One of these is that a particular passage can have reference to a situation unknown to us. Another is that the style is often cryptic and condensed; the author evidently prefers to use as few words as possible. Some sections have an enigmatic character; one can hardly understand these without making careful comparison with other entries or without paying attention to the pattern of the book as a whole. Finally, as regards the poetry in *Markings*, we are sometimes faced with critical difficulties not unlike those which face any careful reader of modern poetry.

Two Retrospections

Hammarskjöld has given us two retrospective surveys of the development of his spiritual life. The first, the radio talk given during his first year at the United Nations, has already been mentioned.[4] The text of this address covers only one and a half pages. However, in this short text he accurately weighed every word, and he has given us a remarkable insight into his spiritual history. The second retrospection is to be found in *Markings* (p.169). It was written on Whitsunday of 1961, and is the last marking that he wrote in prose. This retrospection is even shorter—only twenty-two lines. Nevertheless, it is of the greatest importance, since it

[4] See p. 2 above.

represents his final words on the subject of his spiritual development, and since it was written when his time at the United Nations was nearly over.

In the first retrospection, Hammarskjöld reviews the contributions his parents made to his spiritual heritage. From his father he received "a belief that no life was more satisfactory than one of selfless service to your country—or humanity"; from his mother he received "a belief that, in the very radical sense of the Gospels, all men were equals as children of God, and should be met and treated by us as our masters in God." Concerning the importance of "the beliefs in which I was brought up," he says that they "had given my life direction even when my intellect still challenged their validity."

Hammarskjöld describes the journey on which he refound his religious faith and could recognize these beliefs "as mine in their own right and by my free choice." He emphasizes that prerequisite to this recognition was an understanding of the religious language that he had discovered in his contacts with the medieval mystics: "The language of religion is a set of formulas which register a basic spiritual experience. It must not be regarded as describing, in terms to be defined by philosophy, the reality which is accessible to our senses and which we can analyse with the tools of logic." He was, he says, "late in understanding what this meant."

In the last part of this statement he returns again to the mystics. Before that, however, he acknowledges his debt to Albert Schweitzer at two points: in the ethics of Schweitzer his own inherited ideals had been "harmonized and adjusted to the demands of our world today"; and in the works of Schweitzer he had found "a key for modern man to the world of the Gospels." When he then returns to the mystics he begins with a *but,* showing that he found something in the mystics that he did not find in Schweitzer. He writes: "But the explanation of how man should live a life of active social service in full harmony with himself as a member of the community of the spirit, I found in the writings of those great medieval mystics for whom 'self-surrender' had been the way to self-realization, and who in 'singleness of mind' and 'inwardness' had found strength to say *yes* to every demand which the needs of their neighbors made them face."[5]

[5] Hammarskjöld, "Old Creeds," pp. 23–24.

As far as it goes this retrospection is reliable; it can easily be verified in *Markings*. Yet it simultaneously raises many questions, not least concerning the relative influences of Schweitzer and the mystics. There will be several opportunities in this book to return to these problems; here, however, let me offer some preliminary observations.

Schweitzer meant much to Hammarskjöld, but it must be observed that, according to the retrospection, his influence was mainly at the point of ethical and exegetical questions. Obviously Hammarskjöld is even more grateful to the mystics. But it must be pointed out that he interprets them very much in his own way, departing from more familiar viewpoints. Further, it is important to pay attention to the fact that Hammarskjöld considered the mystics to be of great help both in the *recovery* of Christian faith and in the possible *elucidation* of this faith. One must bear these observations in mind if one is to avoid overestimating either the role of Schweitzer or that of the mystics in Hammarskjöld's development. In fact, overestimations of both kinds are to be found in the literature already produced about *Markings*.

The second retrospection, which dates from 1961, contains at least two statements of utmost importance. The first concerns Hammarskjöld's "yes," a yes that appears often in *Markings*—a yes to God, to himself, and to destiny. In this retrospection from his last Whitsunday we read: "I don't know Who—or what—put the question, I don't know when it was put. I don't even remember answering. But at some moment I did answer *Yes* to Someone—or Something—and from that hour I was certain that existence is meaningful and that, therefore, my life, in self-surrender, had a goal" (p. 169). This declaration contains certain features that might seem peculiar to one who has read the preceding part of *Markings*. The remarkable element here is the vagueness of the expressions used, in sharp contrast to the clarity of the declarations concerning the *yes* which appeared at the beginning of 1953. Here, Hammarskjöld expresses a far-reaching uncertainty concerning both the origin of the question and the recipient of the answer as well as the occasions of the question and the answer. I hope nevertheless to show that this dimness actually helps us better to understand the years of crisis as they appear in *Markings*—and the author's growing yes.

The English text of the second statement in the Whitsunday marking must be altered because the translator has omitted Hammarskjöld's very distinctive and direct reference to Jesus as "the hero of the Gospels." Hammarskjöld actually wrote: "As I continued along the Way, I learned, step by step, word by word, that behind every sentence spoken by the hero of the Gospels, stands *one* man and *one* man's experience. Also behind the prayer that the cup might pass from him and his promise to drink it. Also behind each of the words from the Cross."

The points at which Jesus is directly mentioned in *Markings* are relatively few. However, this declaration from Whitsunday 1961 shows that Jesus had been a permanent companion in Hammarskjöld's religious meditations and that this companionship had influenced in high degree the entire course of the meditations. Two things must again be observed. First, when Hammarskjöld italicizes the word *one*—"*one* man" and "*one* man's experience"—we must remember that *one* and *oneness* are honorary words in *Markings*. The accentuation of *one* can be interpreted to mean Jesus *alone*—Jesus alone as hero of the Gospels. But we must also remember that the words *one* and *oneness* often mean wholeness in contrast to dividedness. The *one* could thus also mean: in him there is no dividedness; he is not double-minded but altogether "whole." Second, let us also observe that when Hammarskjöld in this passage strongly accentuates the cup and the cross he directly and consciously makes this correspond to what, in this same passage, he has already said about his own way: "I came to a time and place where I realized that the Way leads to a triumph which is a catastrophe, and to a catastrophe which is a triumph, that the price for committing one's life would be reproach, and that the only elevation possible to man lies in the depths of humiliation." Throughout the book, *sacrifice* is a fundamental word, but in the author's last years it became more and more prominent. Certainly these words from Whitsunday 1961 do not mean that Hammarskjöld compared his sacrifice with that of Jesus, and still less that he considered himself a new Messiah. Nevertheless, he was convinced that he must reckon with the possibility—and, as he saw it, a likely possibility —that his way would end with a sacrifice of death.

Chapter Two

YEARS OF CRISIS

Answering Yes without Knowing When

In *Markings* Hammarskjöld's first important *yes* appears in full brightness. It is strongly underlined, being the first marking of a New Year—even that year in which his life was radically changed by his election as Secretary General of the United Nations. The passage begins with the same words as do the first markings of the three preceding years: "Night is drawing nigh"—*night* here meaning the end of life—a quotation from a Swedish hymn that, in Hammarskjöld's youth, his mother always read on the eve of each New Year. But in 1953 he continued: "For all that has been—Thanks! To all that shall be—Yes!" (p. 87). The contrast between these words and the last entry of 1952 could hardly be more striking. His New Year's yes from 1953 was to be repeated many times and to become fixed as a yes to God, to himself, and to destiny. His situation, as compared with that of the preceding years, had changed radically —a door to a new world had been opened by this yes.

All of this seems to be very clear. Nevertheless, a question must be raised. It may seem difficult to bring these transparent statements into harmony with the vague statements of Whitsunday 1961. Van Dusen has seen this difficulty, and he has attempted to explain the apparent differences by saying that in 1961 Hammarskjöld had probably not reviewed his writings from earlier years,[1] and that, therefore, in 1961 he could not locate the precise moment of his yes. This explanation, however, is not convincing. Hammarskjöld may well have forgotten much that he had written during the years, but it is unlikely that he could not remember this most remarkable passage of 1953, written only a short time before the

[1] Henry Pitney Van Dusen, *Dag Hammarskjöld: The Statesman and His Faith* (New York: Harper, 1967), p. 100.

great vocational change of his life. There are good reasons for considering the Whitsunday 1961 passage to be a reliable account of the history of his inner life. He could indeed not determine the exact time of his decisive yes. In fact, the statement of 1961 must be interpreted as denying that "the exact time" was to be found in the New Year passage of 1953. The decisive yes had been said earlier—secretly, during the time of Hammarskjöld's hard struggles of mind. The function of the 1953 writing is openly to reveal what had happened in secret at some time in the past that he was not able to fix.

These observations are important from many points of view. First, they show that Hammarskjöld's yes was *not*—as some interpreters have proposed—connected with or even derived from his election as Secretary General. This interpretation points to the fact that the 1953 passage is immediately followed by some undated entries that, evidently, were written during the days when Hammarskjöld, having been informed about the approaching election, was meditating on the possible development of the future. However, such an interpretation is irreconcilable with the fact that Hammarskjöld could not fix the time of his yes, and that the time of that secret yes must have been earlier than the 1953 marking.

In his book *Dag Hammarskjöld: Strictly Personal,* Bo Beskow, the artist, has reviewed his memories of the spring of 1953. Beskow was then preparing a portrait of his friend Hammarskjöld. One day they discussed the international situation and the problem of finding a successor to Trygve Lie. Names were mentioned, but none appeared to be a likely choice. Then it suddenly appeared to Beskow that Hammarskjöld would be the right man. He said so, and Hammarskjöld, laughing, answered: "Nobody is crazy enough to propose me—and I would be crazy to accept."[2] Some days later Beskow read in the morning paper a bold headline: "Dag Hammarskjöld the New Secretary General?" Another sitting for the portrait had been arranged for the same day. Hammarskjöld arrived, punctual as always, but there was no painting that day, only talking. During the days between the sittings Hammarskjöld had received the proposal, and now he was ready to accept. Beskow writes: "I don't think he felt it as a heavy 'duty' to accept—he saw the appoint-

---

[2] Bo Beskow, *Dag Hammarskjöld: Strictly Personal* (Garden City, N.Y.: Doubleday, 1969), p. 12.

ment as a challenge and a chance to do some really useful work. He was pleased and excited."[3] Hammarskjöld no doubt received the election with thankfulness, and to that extent Beskow's view is quite right. But the passages in *Markings* which seem obviously to have been written in the days of his pondering the proposed appointment are, quite naturally, much more complicated. In the light of his faith in God he meditates upon "what had befallen me" (p. 87).

In one of the relevant sections from 1953 we read: "When in decisive moments—as now—God acts, it is with a stern purposefulness, a Sophoclean irony. When the hour strikes, He takes what is His. What have *you* to say? —Your prayer has been answered, as you know. God has a use for you, even though what He asks doesn't happen to suit you at the moment. God, who 'abases him whom He raises up'" (p. 87). This surely implies that Hammarskjöld is able to accept what happens as a gift from God and as an answer to his prayer. It certainly does not imply that Hammarskjöld might have prayed to become Secretary General. His prayer must rather have been like the one from 1952, to find "something to live for, great enough to die for" (p. 85). In the next marking (p. 87) we meet his complicated reactions in regard to the new situation. He begins by quoting the Swedish poet Gunnar Ekelöf: "Will it come, or will it not, / The day when the joy becomes great, / The day when the grief becomes small?" Then he continues: "It *did* come—the day when the grief became small. For what had befallen me and seemed so hard to bear became insignificant in the light of the demands which God was now making. But how difficult it is to feel that this was also, and for that very reason, the day when the joy became great." The crucial phrase in this passage is "the demands God was now making." In the light of these overriding demands the hardness of the charge seemed "insignificant"— therefore the grief became small and, *also,* the joy great. Even after this, however, Hammarskjöld finds it difficult to *feel* the joy that is based on the demands of God.

A very brief entry follows: "Not I, but God in me." Many similar pronouncements appear later in *Markings,* when Hammarskjöld talks about his "mystical experience" and about faith as union with God. The

---

[3] Ibid.

precise meaning of such words will be discussed more thoroughly below. At this point, however, their significance is clearly seen when they are considered in connection with both the preceding and the following passages. Then "God in me" involves the hearing of the inescapable demands of God and, further, the receiving of strength from God. Having spoken about the necessity of being "entirely indifferent to yourself through an absolute assent to your destiny" Hammarskjöld continues to lay bare his journey by describing what strength from God means in relation to men: "He who has placed himself in God's hand stands free vis-à-vis men: he is entirely at his ease with them, because he has granted them the right to judge" (p. 88). Then, on the day of his final decision (April 7, 1953), Hammarskjöld quotes Thomas à Kempis. The main thought of this passage may be expressed aphoristically: Nothing to the glory of men; all to the glory of God—*soli deo gloria*.

Among subsequent entries from 1953 in which Hammarskjöld continues to meditate on what has befallen him I shall mention only two. The first runs: "He who has surrendered himself to it knows that the Way ends on the Cross—even when it is leading him through the jubilation of Gennesaret or the triumphal entry into Jerusalem" (p. 88). This is a meditation in the presence of Christ—a meditation concerning the significance of the discipleship which follows Him on the way of self-surrender. To follow Him means to be prepared to pay the cost. Of course, Hammarskjöld does not think that he will be crucified, but he is contemplating what the "judgment of men" may bring and, being familiar with the biblical sayings concerning the following of Christ, he probably has in mind such passages as: "It is enough for the disciple to be like his teacher, and the servant like his master. If they have called the master of the house Beelzebul, how much more will they malign those of his household" (Matt. 10:25). The second entry to be noted is a declaration of release: "To be free, to be able to stand up and leave *everything* behind—without looking back. To say *Yes*—" (p. 88). These two markings, seen together, display the inner tension of Hammarskjöld's reactions to what "had befallen him." All of these pronouncements from the spring of 1953, now considered, reveal the meaning which his yes, once said in secret, had for him in the time of his life's momentous change.

The fact of this hidden yes and the fact that Hammarskjöld could not indicate a fixed time for it also give us additional important information. We see that in his life there was no sudden "conversion." He does not belong to those who have been called the "twice-born." In his retrospection he talks about "a never abandoned effort frankly and squarely to build up a personal belief in the light of experience and honest thinking."[4] Entries in *Markings* from his years of crisis entirely verify this statement. But they do not only reveal his "efforts"; they say even more. In fact, the relevant passages make it clear that his yes had been a *slowly growing yes*. There are, during this period, a host of statements which indicate Hammarskjöld's inability "to believe." Confessions of such kind—"I cannot believe," "I dare not believe"—continue to appear until the final entry of 1952. Nevertheless, there are also more than a few entries which indicate how the light broke through his darkness. From this point of view it is quite understandable that it really was impossible for him to fix the "moment" of his yes. That being the case, Hammarskjöld, when looking back, could not but consider his own free yes as a gift from the God who —as he says—had seized him: "Long ago, you gripped me, Slinger" (p.134).

Tormenting Questions

Hammarskjöld's "negotiations with himself" written before 1953 reveal a continual self-examination. With a radical frankness he unmasks his inner life and, acting as his own judge, mercilessly condemns all that he considers intolerable—a judgment that, in reality, is not only a condemnation of different traits and attitudes, but a condemnation of his entire self. Obviously, his way of expressing himself brings forth much which tempts psychological analysis. However, even if some psychological aspects must necessarily be kept in view, it is not my intention to do psychological or "depth-psychological" research. I am concerned primarily with analyzing how Hammarskjöld himself looked upon the questions which tormented him in this time of his life.

Yet, before I take up these problems, it may be suitable to present some general observations about Hammarskjöld's origins and the circumstances

---

[4] Dag Hammarskjöld, "Old Creeds in a New World," in *Servant of Peace,* ed. Wilder Foote (New York: Harper, 1962), p. 23.

during the twenties at Uppsala, where he spent his youth and student years. As has already been pointed out, he himself very strongly accentuated the important role of his paternal and, not less, his maternal inheritance. Without doubt, his relations to his father were complicated in a way that his relations to his mother never were. But no matter how intricate may have been his relations to the strong and powerfully effective Hjalmar Hammarskjöld—formerly Prime Minister of Sweden (1914-17) and at the time of Dag's academic studies Governor in Uppsala—Dag always gratefully acknowledged the ideals of life encountered in his father as well as in his entire paternal tradition. Those ideals are best summed up in the words *duty, righteousness,* and *selfless service.* Such ideals were not only a starting point for Dag Hammarskjöld; they also became permanent companions throughout his life. His mother Agnes had a warm, deep, and unsophisticated piety—a piety that never brooded upon theological or philosophical questions, being more accurately described as the piety of a practising faith which, with all-embracing kindness, endeavored as much as possible to help men in need. There is no need to explain what his mother's living and active faith meant to Dag. Certainly, his way to faith—or back to faith—was a way of hard brooding. But he had seen at closest quarters what authentic faith was, and he could never forget that impression.

Dag Hammarskjöld in 1954 succeeded his father as one of the eighteen members of the Swedish Academy—an event unique in his history of the academy. In his inaugural address he spoke of the situation in Uppsala in the twenties. Europe's strange, brief idyll between the two wars had had, he declared, "a reflection all its own in Upsala. The church policy of Söderblom in this period made the city an international center. Söderblom and Hjalmar Hammarskjöld joyfully shared the burden of the ceremonial tasks which accompanied this development."[5]

At the point of religion the Uppsala of the 1920s was stretched in tension between two poles. On one side there was an intense activity in matters ecclesiastical and theological, led chiefly by the archbishop, Nathan Söderblom, a man of most remarkable initiative and innovation. On the other side there was the celebrated "Uppsala school" of philos-

[5] Dag Hammarskjöld, "Hjalmar Hammarskjöld," in *Servant of Peace* (see n. 4 above), pp. 77-78.

ophy, led chiefly by Professor Axel Hägerström, whose academic work was marked by a critical attitude towards religion, an attitude that—rightly or wrongly—was most frequently seen as hostile towards Christian faith. The highly intellectual Hammarskjöld could not escape the critical views of this school of philosophical analysis; indeed, the Uppsala philosophy was instrumental in exciting the crisis apparent in *Markings*. His retrospective statement of 1953 was doubtless connected with this academic ferment. It was a true liberation when he discovered that religious language is primarily the registration of a "basic spiritual experience" and "must not be regarded as describing, in terms to be defined by philosophy, the reality which is accessible to our senses and which we can analyze with the tools of logic."[6] This statement not only tells us about his personal liberation; it must also be seen as a testimony to his struggles with—and his indebtedness to—the Uppsala school of philosophy.

Intimate relations between the castle of the governor and the residence of the archbishop existed in the Uppsala of the 1920s and, no doubt, this relationship meant much to Dag Hammarskjöld. Due primarily to the enormous efforts of Söderblom, the first ecumenical assembly on "Life and Work" convened in Stockholm in 1925. Through that assembly Dag Hammarskjöld made his first contact with the worldwide community. When in 1954, as Secretary General, he addressed the Second Assembly of the World Council of Churches in Evanston, Illinois, he looked back to events of the twenties, saying: "As a student I saw at close quarters the beginning of the great ecumenical movement, and I learned to admire one of its inspired leaders, Archbishop Nathan Söderblom."[7]

However, there are other observations to be made concerning Hammarskjöld's years in Uppsala. In reviewing his spiritual development he acknowledges his debt to Albert Schweitzer and "the great medieval mystics." Why Schweitzer? Why the mystics? These questions have often been raised, and different answers have been given. It is worthwhile, in this connection, to remember the close relations betwen Schweitzer and Uppsala in the twenties. When, after World War I, his hospital in Africa encountered heavy economic problems, Schweitzer

---

[6] Hammarskjöld, "Old Creeds," p. 23.
[7] Dag Hammarskjöld, "An Instrument of Faith," in *Servant of Peace* (see n. 4 above), p. 56.

received aid from Söderblom who, among other things, arranged organ concerts in Sweden for the prominent interpreter of Bach. Further, Schweitzer was invited to Uppsala as "Olaus Petri Lecturer," and there delivered a series of most distinguished lectures. Schweitzer was well known everywhere in Sweden, and not least in Uppsala. Dag Hammarskjöld probably became interested in Schweitzer at an early stage.

Concerning the medieval mystics, it must be remembered that in the 1920s the study of mysticism was rather a fashion in many European countries. In Uppsala Söderblom had contributed to this study by producing several books on mysticism. He attempted to distinguish between two different kinds of mysticism: the "mysticism of infinitude" and the "mysticism of personality." Söderblom's theory was much discussed, and Hammarskjöld had ample opportunity for contact with the study of mysticism. Of course, these observations do not explain why Hammarskjöld ultimately turned to Schweitzer and the mystics for help; they show, however, how natural it might have been for Hammarskjöld to seek their aid in his need.

We turn now to the problems that tormented Hammarskjöld during his long time of religious crisis. From an external point of view these years were years of personal prosperity. He advanced rapidly to important offices, finally becoming a minister in the Swedish cabinet. His abilities were more and more esteemed; his capacity for dealing effectively with difficult affairs was widely known. It is almost inconceivable that at the same time the inner life of this fortunate, self-possessed, and polished man was like a turbulent sea.

His spiritual struggles, as they are revealed in *Markings,* revolved around three predominant issues: self-centeredness, loneliness, and the meaninglessness of life. To be sure, these three issues cannot be distinctly separated from each other; they belong intimately together and, indeed, often shade into each other. Nevertheless, each issue has something of its own to say concerning the total problem tormenting the author of the diary. If a critique of self-centeredness stands at the outset of his analysis, it is a meaningless life which must surely be seen as the virtually inevitable consequence of that attitude. It must be acknowledged, moreover, that self-centeredness is in some form a constant companion to all spiritual anxiety. And further: although loneliness and meaninglessness —or, to use a more current term, alienation—appear to belong in a special way to the mood of our time, as so much "modern literature" indicates, the issues themselves have surely been familiar to all ages.

Self-centeredness. A constitutive element of Hammarskjöld's life was his intense demand or, as he himself says, his "hunger" for righteousness and purity of mind. It was within the framework of this hunger that he examined himself, and the result was a relentless and ruthless self-critique. A few passages from *Markings* show the quality of his critique and indicate its concentration on self-centeredness. He persistently feels judgment over his life: "Day by day, / You suffer anguish, / Anguish under the unspoken judgment which hangs over your life, / While leaves fall in the fool's paradise" (p. 51). He compares his life to a blown egg: "A blown egg floats well, and sails well on every puff of wind—light enough for such performances, since it has become nothing but shell, with neither embryo nor nourishment for its growth" (p. 52). Accusations of these kinds he combines with and derives from accusations of selfishness: " 'Ego-love' contains an element of gourmandise which our language lacks the right cadences to express: *Mon cher moi— âme et corps—tu me fais un grand plaisir!* Your ego-love doesn't bloom unless it is sheltered. The rules are simple: don't commit yourself to any one and, therefore, don't allow anyone to come close to you. Simple—and fateful. Its efforts to shelter its love create a ring of cold around the Ego which slowly eats its way inwards towards the core" (p. 54).

The questions Hammarskjöld asks himself do not concern only certain isolated or individual mistakes and shortcomings; they concern the self as a whole: "It is not the repeated mistakes, the long succession of petty betrayals—though, God knows, they would give cause enough for anxiety and self-contempt—but the huge elementary mistake, the betrayal of that within me which is greater than I—in a complacent adjustment to alien demands" (p. 57). Self-centeredness kills the sentiment for others: "Do you really have 'feelings' any longer for anybody or anything except yourself—or even that? Without the strength of a personal commitment, your experience of others is at most aesthetic. Yet, today, even such a maimed experience brought you into touch with a portion of spiritual reality which revealed your utter poverty" (p. 58). This negative attitude to others is often repeated—as, for instance, when he portrays himself as an arrogant pusher. With self-ironical sarcasm he says: "As a climber you will have a wide sphere of activity even after, if that should happen, you reach your goal. You can, for instance, try to prevent others from becoming better qualified than yourself" (p. 75). Even when the ugliness of self-love is recognized it holds its grip: "Narcissus leant over the spring, enchanted by his own ugliness, which he prided himself upon having the courage to admit" (p. 68). Then he contemplates the demonic character of self-centeredness: "The ride on the Witches' Sabbath to the Dark Tower where we meet only ourselves, ourselves, ourselves" (p. 68). As a result of his self-examination Hammarskjöld can provide a summary in the following statement, where, obviously, the first words refer to what is said about Jesus in John 2:25, a reference missed in the English translation of *Markings:* "He . . . needed no one to bear witness of man; for he himself knew what was in man." The English passage ought to be: "Out of his own self he [Jesus] knew—I know what man is: vulgarity, lust, pride, envy—and longing. Longing—also for the Cross" (p. 65*). Sayings such as these disclose not only Hammarskjöld's self-contempt but also the contempt for others which he frequently enunciates in *Markings:* "At any rate, your contempt for your fellow human beings does not prevent you, with a well-guarded self-respect, from trying to win their respect" (p. 53). In a more complicated entry he observes that aggressive feelings of contempt can be hidden within such an attempt: "Out of loyalty to others he was compelled to be aggressive by *their* feelings of inferiority" (p. 67).

These passages, which could be complemented by many others, demonstrate the openness and ruthlessness of his self-examination. In a well-known and very expressive statement Martin Luther describes sin as life which is *incurvatus in se*. Hammarskjöld's "negotiations with himself" must clearly be understood as a many-sided and thoroughgoing interpretation of what it means to be curved into the ego. His diary of "Road Marks" proves how he fights his self-centeredness and how he relentlessly hunts it down to its most secret hiding places.

Loneliness. One of Hammarskjöld's markings combines the demand for righteousness with a demand for fellowship. This passage can serve as a transition when, now, our attention is directed to the problem of loneliness. Hammarskjöld writes: "Hunger is my native place in the land of the passions. Hunger for fellowship, hunger for righteousness—for a fellowship founded on righteousness, and a righteousness attained in fellowship" (p.62). His confessions of loneliness must be seen from different, but profoundly human, aspects: the renouncement of marriage, social relations, friends. Nevertheless, this human aspect does not stand alone.

Concerning the question of marriage and his failure to enter into that state, a statement from 1952 seems to be decisive:

> Incapable of being blinded by desire,
> Feeling I have no right to intrude upon another,
> Shy of exposing my own nakedness,
> Demanding complete accord as a condition for a life together:
> How could things have gone otherwise? (p. 85*)

Here Hammarskjöld speaks of himself as "shy," and, no doubt, a certain shyness and reservedness belonged to his nature. However, in respect to human relationships the question of the meaning of his loneliness is a rather complicated one. Certainly, he criticizes—often and with vigor—the normal forms of social intercourse. But that does not mean that he was antisocial or without friends. He was not. There are myriad testimonies to the contrary, evidences of a remarkable ability for social communication. He had no difficulty in cooperating with fellow workers and, no doubt, here he found many associates whom he himself would describe as friends in the usual sense of the word. Also, his life was always marked by friendships of a more intimate kind. On the other hand, however, his demand for friendship which was worth its name was apparently very far-reaching and, seemingly, imposed standards that could hardly be met. It is significant that, as far as we know, he never talked openly to anyone—except Leif Belfrage, to whom he addressed himself most cryptically—about his diary and its contents. What he wrote there was a secret kept to himself. Thus his loneliness, we must say, was a chosen one. In the passage that concludes his most remarkable meditation before the Gospels' picture of Jesus he writes: "Compelled or chosen—in the end, the vista of future loneliness only allows a choice between two alternatives: either to despair in desolation, or to stake so high on the 'possibility' that one acquires the right to life in a communion beyond the individual. But doesn't choosing the second call for the kind of faith which moves mountains?" (p. 73*). It is not to be denied that later, during his tenure as Secretary General, his loneliness was very much compelled. Nevertheless it was also, during all his life, in some degree a chosen loneliness.

In terms, however, of the meaning of loneliness in *Markings* it is definitely not sufficient to take into account only human relationships. In fact, loneliness has far deeper roots. It can be described as a cosmic loneliness, or, still more to the point, as a loneliness in respect to existence as a whole. The horror of loneliness: "The anguish of loneliness brings blasts from the storm center of death" (p. 51). A cosmic perspective appears in an entry that describes life in a mine: "At the head of the narrow adit, lit only by the searchlight of the mechanical shovel which bites through the rock like the jaws of a caterpillar. Continual darkness. The same continual cold, dripping with moisture. The same continual loneliness—hemmed in by walls or rock, but without the safety of a wall" (p. 49). The existential perspective:

> The longest journey
> Is the journey inwards.
> Of him who has chosen his destiny,
> Who has started upon his quest
> For the source of his being
> (Is there a source?).
> He is still with you,
> But without relation,
> Isolated in your feeling
> Like one condemned to death
> Or one whom imminent farewell
> Prematurely dedicates
> To the loneliness which is the final lot of all. (p. 65.)

These passages bear a stamp of despair. Yet there is also an entry from this same period which hints at a more positive aspect: "He is one of those who has had the wilderness for a pillow, and called a star his brother. Alone. But loneliness can be a communion" (p. 52). The "he" of this marking is both the writer and, at the same time, a visionary figure. The writer knows that human loneliness can be joined to communion with that which is otherworldly, but this is still a knowledge without experience, a knowledge based on vision, a proleptic sign of the change to come. Yet Hammarskjöld's final marking concerning loneliness from this time, the last entry from 1952, runs: "Loneliness is not the sickness unto death. No, but can it be cured except by death? And does it not become the harder to bear the closer one comes to death?" (p. 86).

The meaninglessness of life. A main feature of the markings, during the time of crisis, is Hammarskjöld's hard struggle to find life meaningful. This seems to be a hunt for a phantom which is constantly flying and disappearing from sight. "A modest wish: that our doings and dealings may be of a little more significance to life than a man's dinner jacket is to his digestion. Yet not a little of what we describe as our achievement is, in fact, no more than a garment in which, on festive occasions, we seek to hide our nakedness" (p. 53). Success is unable to give any satisfactory answer to the question of meaninglessness: "Never let success hide its emptiness from you, achievement its nothingness, toil its desolation. And so keep alive the incentive to push on further, that pain in the soul which drives us beyond ourselves. Whither? That I don't know. That I don't ask to know" (p. 63). When Hammarskjöld reads about persons long dead, he translates history into his own presence: "I am reading about us, as *we* shall be when we are the past. . . . We appear as rather stupid, foolish, self-seeking puppets, moved by obvious strings, which, now and again, get tangled up. It is no caricature that I encounter in the distorting mirror of historical research. Simply the proof that it has all been vanity" (p. 62). Vanity is—as in Ecclesiastes—the final verdict about the history of mankind.

This strong feeling of meaninglessness, leading to despair, provokes an impulse towards self-destruction and suicide. But Hammarskjöld dismisses such a way out as treachery: "Fatigue dulls the pain, but awakes enticing thoughts of death. So! *that* is the way in which you are tempted to overcome your loneliness—by making the ultimate escape from life. —No. It may be that death is to be your ultimate gift to life: it must not be an act of treachery against it" (p. 85). And so the grief of his meditations about the emptiness of life cannot stop him from seeking meaning, even though he is quite aware of the absurdity of his demands: "What I ask for is absurd: that life shall have a meaning. What I strive for is impossible: that my life shall acquire a meaning. I dare not believe, I do not see how I shall ever be able to believe: that I am not alone" (p. 87). Such questions cause him to consider himself ridiculous. A youth of seventeen speaking about "meaning" is—he says—ridiculous; he does not know what he is talking about. "Now, at the age of forty-seven, I am ridiculous because my knowledge of exactly what I am putting down on paper does not stop me from doing so" (p. 86). These are Hammarskjöld's final words about meaninglessness from that time when he saw no meaning at all in life.

A Growing Yes

The passages from *Markings* which we have considered have a dark color, sometimes black as night. Yet there are also other colors to be found in these writings from the time of crisis. It must be observed that Hammarskjöld never felt uncertainty concerning his ethical ideal and its claims. A strong sense of duty, an inescapable view of life as an obligation for the service of men and a constant awareness of responsibility were always firm and unfaltering demands which were never to be questioned. Simultaneously, however, from a religious point of view these years were a period of struggle and skepticism characterized, as he said in retrospect, by "a never abandoned effort frankly and squarely to build up a personal belief in the light of experience and honest thinking."[8] *Markings* drives us to two conclusions concerning these efforts: Hammarskjöld was quite aware of what faith in God both meant and did not mean; further, there are not a few gleams of light which break through the gloom of his torment. To be sure, these gleams are most frequently countersigned by question marks—nevertheless they possess remarkable eloquence.

Entries in Hammarskjöld's diary from as early as 1941–42 show how he recognized faith in God not primarily as assent to statements about God but, rather, as a personal, existential relation. A word about prayer:

[8] Hammarskjöld, "Old Creeds," p. 23.

"Your cravings as a human animal do not become a prayer just because it is God whom you ask to attend to them" (p. 34)— that is, prayer is not authentic simply because God is formally addressed. A word about the necessity of listening to God: "How can you expect to keep your powers of hearing when you never want to listen? That God should have time for you, you seem to take as much for granted as that you cannot have time for Him" (p. 34). Finally, a word telling us that the nearness of God is at once fascinating and tremendous, a *mysterium fascinosum et tremendum:* "On the bookshelf of life, God is a useful work of reference, always at hand but seldom consulted. In the whitewashed hour of birth, He is a jubilation and a refreshing wind, too immediate for memory to catch. But when we are compelled to look ourselves in the face—then He rises above us in terrifying reality, beyond all argument and 'feeling,' stronger than all self-defensive forgetfulness" (p. 37). These words were written before his struggle had reached its most critical stage. Thus, even at the starting point of the intensified strife, Hammarskjöld knew very well that "faith in God" would lose meaning if it were not, primarily, a personal, existential relation to Him.

In 1950–52 Hammarskjöld fought his hardest spiritual battle. Passages from 1950 and 1951 are extraordinarily numerous, while those from 1952 are comparatively few. Our impression is that for a time he held his breath and that there was an interval before a clear yes suddenly appeared at the beginning of 1953. From this period emanate his most gloomy and despairing writings, although also to be found are a considerable number of passages which witness to what I would describe as a growing yes. Here I shall examine certain of these, reserving consideration of others to a later occasion, when we shall investigate the influence on Hammarskjöld of Schweitzer, the medieval mystics, and his own meditations before Christ.

At the outset, let us observe two statements from 1950. The first runs: "God does not die on the day when we cease to believe in a personal deity, but we die on the day when our lives cease to be illumined by the steady radiance, renewed daily, of a wonder, the source of which is beyond all reason" (p. 64). Here we see that he hesitates to speak of God as a person: God—or the Divine—is presented as a "source" from which a radiance of wonder emanates. This statement calls to mind the later retrospection from Whitsunday 1961, where it is said: "I don't know Who—or what—put the question" (p. 169). In the very next passage, having in mind the ethical demand as it appears in Kantian dress, Hammarskjöld still speaks of a divine element in an anonymous way, although he also, as the passage progresses, makes it quite plain that the "subject" in question, operative in him, is at the same time "outside and above" him. He writes: " 'Treat others as ends, never as means.' And myself as an end only in my capacity as a means: to shift the dividing line in my being between subject and object to a position where the subject, even if it is in me, is outside and above me—so that my *whole* being may become an instrument for that which is greater than I" (p.64). This statement suggests what he later says directly about God and his relation to Him. The notion of a subject who is above returns in a writing of 1952 that begins by quoting the words "Thy will be done" from the Our Father. Having admitted that self-interest has been allowed "to supply the energy" in his efforts for others, Hammarskjöld continues: "—no matter, provided only that you allow the final outcome to be decided entirely over your head, in faith" (p. 82).

Similarly, it can be shown that there are many other passages which in different ways preview the future and show that—in spite of the great change in Hammarskjöld's life—much more of a continuity existed than might have been expected. I shall add one or two verifications. In his later period Hammarskjöld makes frequent use of the crucial formula, "not to look back"—as, for instance, in his short retrospection from Whitsunday 1961, where he implies that on account of the *yes* he once said he now knows what it means not to look back. However, this expression appeared early in the time of crisis: "There is a point at which everything becomes simple and there is no longer any question of choice, because all you have staked will be lost if you look back. Life's point of no return" (p. 70). These words, drawn from the Bible, obviously had a rich significance for Hammarskjöld. From one point of view he saw them as liberating, giving him a new freedom. From another point of view he saw them as accentuating the importance of the present moment, the *now*. Such an accent, which was later to become a main feature in *Markings*, we find in an entry from about the same time as the one just quoted: "The present moment is significant, not as the bridge between past and future, but by reason of its contents, contents which can fill our emptiness and become ours, if we are capable of receiving them" (p. 67). The attitude to life here expressed does not mean that Hammarskjöld was a child of the moment, of the flying instant. This attitude has a far deeper significance. It not only stresses the weight that every moment bears from the point of view of present activity, it also implies that eternity is hidden in the moment, there to be discovered.

In two writings from the end of 1951 we meet the expression, "at the frontier of the unheard-of." I shall examine the first of these passages. First, however, the words of a preceding statement should be looked at:

> Low down in cool space
> One star—
> The morning star.
> In the pale light of sparseness
> Lives the Real Thing,
> And we are real. (p. 75)

The morning star here must be viewed as a sign along the way, an idea important for an understanding of the passage, which affirms that the wanderer has arrived at the frontier of a new land: "Now. When I have overcome my fears—of others, of myself, of the underlying darkness: at the frontier of the unheard-of. Here ends the known. But, from a source beyond it, something fills my being with its possibilities. Here desire is purified and made lucid: each action is a preparation for, each choice a *yes* [italics mine] to the unknown. Prevented by the duties of life on the surface from looking down into the depths, yet all the while being slowly trained and molded by them to take the plunge into the deep whence rises the fragrance of a forest star, bearing the promise of a new affinity. At the frontier—" (p. 77*).

This entry shows that the yes is on the way. Earlier, Hammarskjöld had spoken about his situation as a time of expectation—a time of endless waiting, like the experience of children before Christmas. But now he had arrived at a frontier—the end of the known, a point where "the unheard-of" was within reach and, indeed, was already filling him with its "possibilities." There is scarcely need to explain "the unheard-of" or "that which transcends all imagination" (as the Swedish word also could be translated). This is obviously what Hammarskjöld later described as the mystical experience: "to be in the hands of God" (p. 93).

Most remarkable among the intimations of growing light is an entry in *Markings* from 1952. The first words are immediately significant: "Now you know. When the worries over your work loosen their grip, then this experience of light, warmth, and power. From without—a sustaining element, like air to the glider or water to the swimmer. An intellectual hesitation which demands proofs and logical demonstration prevents me from 'believing'—in this, too. Prevents me from constructing it in terms of knowledge as an interpretation of reality. Yet, through me there flashes this vision of a magnetic field in the soul, created in a timeless present by unknown multitudes, living in holy obedience, whose words and actions are a timeless prayer. —'The Communion of Saints'—and—within it—an eternal life" (p. 84*).

Here Hammarskjöld talks openly and in an illuminating way about an experience which can be characterized as a vision. It is a striking feature that his vision appears here and now as an experience of the "communion of saints"; and it is a vision which can be characterized only most impressively: "whose words and actions are *a timeless prayer.*" This theme, like that of eternal life, turns up only rarely in *Markings*. And even in this entry a restriction is to be found: an intellectual hesitation prevents Hammarskjöld from "believing"—the quotation marks are his own—and from giving an analysis or description in terms of knowledge. The point is that he faced intellectual difficulties, and it will be appropriate to investigate those difficulties. Briefly, however, let us first consider the role nature plays in *Markings*.

Throughout the ages philosophers and theologians have often spoken of a "revelation" in nature, and it is worthwhile to look at some statements in *Markings* from that point of view. As is well known, Hammarskjöld was a great lover of nature, and this love is apparent in many of his writings, not only in *Markings*. Nature was for him a permanent source of refreshment, and he never tired of writing of its beauties. But his relation to nature was not only aesthetic; it meant more to him. His reactions and feelings before nature bear an affinity to what he later says—in terms borrowed from the mystics—about faith as "one in the

Unity." Thus in 1958 he wrote: "In the point of rest at the center of our being, we encounter a world where all things are at rest in the same way. Then a tree becomes a mystery, a cloud a revelation, each man a cosmos of whose riches we can only catch glimpses" (p. 148). In his earlier meditations it is clear that nature, acting as a kind of "revelation," helped in Hammarskjöld's struggle to overcome his sense of alienation from existence. It is significant that the most relevant passages in *Markings* concerning the importance of nature were written in his final years of crisis, 1951 and 1952.

Let us scrutinize four of these passages. The first is the testimony of a not satisfied yearning. Having talked about the intercourse of heaven and earth in nature, and having compared this meeting with an embrace between husband and wife, he continues: "I feel an ache of longing to share in this embrace, to be united and absorbed. A longing like carnal desire, but directed towards earth, water, sky, and returned by the whispers of the trees, the fragrance of the soil, the caresses of the wind, the embrace of water and light. Content? No, no, no—but refreshed, rested—while waiting" (p. 78). Soon thereafter he characterizes the experience of great nature as something "extrahuman," saying that we miss the point of this experience "unless we each find a way to chime in as one note in the organic whole" (p. 79). In the third passage he meditates before autumn's dying nature—later to be described as "a dying which is a hymn." He confesses his solidarity with nature, even dying: "Autumn in the wilderness: life as an end in itself, even in the annihilation of the individual life, the distant vistas clear, the neighborhood calm, at the moment of its extinction—this evening I would say Yes to the execution squad, not out of exhaustion or defiance, but with a bright faith in solidarity. To sustain this faith in my life among men" (p. 80*). Finally, Hammarskjöld is quite aware that these experiences of nature involve traces of pantheism: "When the sense of the earth unites with the sense of one's body, one becomes earth of the earth, a plant among plants, an animal born from the soil and fertilizing it. In this union, the body is confirmed in its pantheism" (p. 84).

Such passages as these lay bare the deep meaning which nature held for Hammarskjöld. It is clear, furthermore, that nature played a supporting role in the hardest days of his spiritual struggle.

Intellectual Difficulties

As a conclusion to our study of Hammarskjöld's "years of crisis" it is appropriate that we consider his own analysis of the intellectual difficulties he encountered in respect to the question of faith. We have already seen that his writings from these years openly disclose intensely personal issues: self-centeredness, loneliness, meaninglessness. To be sure, it is not possible to draw boundaries between these kinds of issues; obviously, intellectual difficulties can be intensely personal. Let us—in a general way, at this point, and with these reservations in mind—review certain of the philosophical and theological questions that seem to have vexed Hammarskjöld particularly.

Markings is strikingly replete with declarations concerning the tribulations of Hammarskjöld's inner life, and also strikingly devoid of long speculations concerning philosophy or theology. This is, it must be remembered, a book of confession, not an academic treatise. Nevertheless we can catch glimpses of intellectual problems, chiefly in those entries in the diary which bear a polemical stamp. Such entries are few—Hammarskjöld, in contrast to Schweitzer, was no controversialist—but it is nevertheless worthwhile to contemplate those passages which he wrote with the sting of polemics.

The years of crisis were a time of skepticism. Even when, in clear and expressive words, Hammarskjöld talks about his "experiences" or his "visions," there are always reservations. He cannot—as he says in a passage already quoted—overcome an intellectual hesitation, a demand for proofs and logical demonstration which prevents him from interpreting, in terms of knowledge, his own experience as a construct of reality. Demands of that kind were endemic to the philosophy of the Uppsala school which dominated during Hammarskjöld's university years. According to that philosophy, religion belonged to the world of "feeling," and therefore it was impossible to consider religion an interpretation of "reality." Attempts to cast religion in terms of reality lead inevitably to a metaphysics which, from a scientific point of view, must be strongly opposed as purely meaningless. Hammarskjöld was, as we have seen, familiar with the ideas of this philosophical school and with its critical attitude—all of which, no doubt, contributed to the skepticism of his writings.

In his retrospection of 1953 Hammarskjöld describes how a new insight concerning the character of religious language helped to relieve him of such philosophical difficulties. The force of this new insight was that religious language "is a set of formulas which register a basic spiritual experience" and that that language "must not be regarded as describing, in terms to be defined by philosophy, the reality which is accessible to our senses and which we can analyse with the tools of logic."[9] This statement is, to be sure, akin to the view of the Uppsala philosophy that religious language describes "feelings"; for Hammarskjöld, however, it was never a matter of reducing the issue of faith to the question of "feelings." Statements in *Markings* show abundantly that, when talking about God, his intention was to assert a contact with a "reality," even the "ultimate reality."

Hammarskjöld's new view of religious language raises at least two important points. First, this "ultimate reality" is not available to a logical analysis of the world of sense. It is beyond reason; it is the "unheard-of," a mystery. In a most interesting passage, Hammarskjöld criticizes a caricature of faith: "There is a pride of faith, more unforgivable and dangerous than the pride of the intellect. It reveals a split personality in which faith is 'observed' and appraised, thus negating that unity born of a dying-unto-self, which is the definition of faith. To 'value' faith is to turn it into a metaphysical magic, the advantages of which ought to be reserved for a spiritual elite" (p. 97). The main intention of this view is to emphasize the humility of faith. However, it is by no accident that Hammarskjöld in this connection talks about "metaphysical magic." Apparently he thinks that pride and speaking about God in a metaphysical way somehow belong together; both tend—somehow or other—to put God at one's own disposal. Against such a caricature of faith, describable only as such, Hammarskjöld strongly insists on the mystery of faith unattainable to metaphysical speculation. In this connection, it ought to be observed that Hammarskjöld, as far as he is fighting "metaphysical magic," is quite in harmony with the Uppsala philosophy.

A second point of importance is that man does not have adequate expressions to use when trying to describe what faith in God means. "Faith *is:* it cannot, therefore, be comprehended, far less identified with

[9] Ibid.

the formulae in which we paraphrase what is" (p. 91*). From this point of view Hammarskjöld is suspicious about the use of anthropomorphisms. We have already observed how in an early entry he discussed the word *person* in respect to God, and we shall listen again to such discussions. Yet he does, in addressing God, use *Thou,* the most intimate of all personal pronouns. But talking to God in such a personal manner did not for him mean accepting "person" as an adequate attribute. In fact, he considered the use of all "anthropocentric" attributes, with respect to God, inadequate and open to misunderstanding; even the focal attribute *love* is, he says, a "very misused and misinterpreted word." Nevertheless, if the use of such attributes seems to be simultaneously inadequate and meaningful, then our speech about God must be characterized as *symbolic*. This is an insight true to Hammarskjöld's meaning, even though he does not use the term.

No doubt, this insight concerning the meaning of religious language provided Hammarskjöld with great release. Faith in God means primarily a personal, existential relationship, not an assent to fixed doctrines. Statements about God—so far as they can be articulated—are statements about the God who makes himself known in the relationship of faith without thereby ceasing to be a mystery. In an early writing, from 1942, where Hammarskjöld has spoken of self-knowledge as a prerequisite "to grasp what faith is," he continues: "How many have been driven into outer darkness by empty talk about faith as an assent to doctrines" (p. 37*). For Hammarskjöld this polemical statement is remarkably rigorous. "Empty talk"—a description of a speech that does not understand either faith or its problems. There is no point in presenting a list of doctrines to people in search of faith, or in demanding the acceptance of a catalogue of dogmas. The effect of such action may easily be "outer darkness." We can ask: Is Hammarskjöld here alluding to difficulties that he himself has experienced? The answer may to some degree be affirmative, for he had not escaped being confronted with such a presentation—or, rather, concealment—of the problems. However, it is also possible that here he has in mind others whose shipwrecks of faith he had witnessed. At any rate he was never, even in the hardest of his inner struggles, "driven into outer darkness." Further, in his academic work at Uppsala, when Nathan Söderblom was the dominant figure in church and theology, Hammarskjöld had had the problems of Christian faith presented in ways quite different from those typical of the narrow-minded doctrinairism against which he wrote so sharply. In fact, even his very early writings show—as we already know—that long before he uttered his *yes,* he was fully aware of the meaning of faith in God as primarily a personal and existential relationship. Thus his new insight concerning religious language was actually a help in the clarification of thoughts which he had long had, although he had not recognized their full significance and consequences.

If, however, this fundamental insight concerning the nature of religious language was for Hammarskjöld a liberation, it neither made him indifferent to the contents of intellectual problems nor served to dissolve those problems. On the contrary, we shall see how in *Markings* it is continually proven that he was always wrestling with problems of a theological character. He was, of course, not a professional scholar whose particular vocational obligation was to contemplate all manner of theological questions. His problems were only those that had personal importance. This fact, to be sure, does not reduce our interest in his expositions; our interest is rather increased by the knowledge that all of his problems were treated in a very personal way and in the manner of a highly intellectual man not trained in academic theology. Not least is it interesting to see *how* Hammarskjöld treated difficulties which appeared when he encountered confessional statements which had arisen in the history of Christianity. His insight into the significance of religious language tended to make his attitude neither doctrinaire nor merely negative. It was necessary that his aim always be to discover the religious values hidden behind the confessional statements. He was clearly no controversialist in the usual sense of that word. His writings show no interest in the party conflicts of opposing theological schools. He was here, as in his political behavior, no party man. This attitude, however, never prevented Hammarskjöld from stating his opinions clearly and distinctly— nor from engaging in strong criticism when on occasion his writings assumed polemical form.

Chapter Three

HELP ON THE WAY

Albert Schweitzer

When in the first chapter we considered Hammarskjöld's two retrospective reviews of his spiritual development, we found him acknowledging his gratitude for help that had come to him on his way from skepticism to an unambiguous confession of a Christian faith. In the first retrospection he mentions Albert Schweitzer and "the great medieval mystics." And in the important Whitsunday 1961 marking he speaks of perpetual meditations before "the hero of the Gospels." Now we shall examine in greater detail the actual benefit Hammarskjöld derived from these sources of stimulation and help. It is most appropriate that we begin with an investigation of his relation to Albert Schweitzer.

As we have seen, Hammarskjöld even in his student days had broad opportunity for contact with Schweitzer and his work. In the twenties Schweitzer lectured in Uppsala concerning his "philosophy of life," and his writings were at that time much discussed in Sweden. It is not surprising that these writings engaged students like Hammarskjöld who were wrestling with ethical and religious problems. Hammarskjöld's interest in Schweitzer was, to be sure, stimulated by the unusual and rather sensational manner of the man's life. Here was a man already famous throughout the intellectual world for his striking and revolutionary exegetical research, who had suddenly left not only university life but also Western civilization as such for elementary medical work in the forests of Africa, his intention being thereby to repay a farthing of the immense debt of the white man to the black. This manner of life Hammarskjöld admired in explicit terms: Schweitzer was to him "a living example of the ethics he proclaimed." Hammarskjöld expressed this attitude towards Schweitzer in an article published in Sweden in 1951 and in correspondence with Schweitzer during his tenure at the United Nations.

It is worth recalling that Hammarskjöld, when speaking about Schweitzer, accentuated two important things he had derived from Schweitzer—two gifts: a comprehensive ethical view of life, and "the key for modern man to the world of the Gospels." We shall speak of this "key" later when we examine Hammarskjöld's meditations before "the hero of the Gospels." Here we shall concentrate our attention on Schweitzer's ethical philosophy and its meaning for Hammarskjöld.

In *Markings* there are many quotations from the medieval mystics, but not a single one from Schweitzer. Nor do we anywhere discover the watchword which Schweitzer used to characterize his philosophy: "Reverence for Life." Nevertheless there are many points in *Markings* which clearly indicate the influence of Schweitzer. They are to be found chiefly in the first part of the book, before 1953, although later passages also reveal the figure of Schweitzer.

In 1942 Hammarskjöld wrote: "Our secret creative will divines its counterpart in others, experiencing its own universality, and this intuition builds a road towards knowledge of the power which is itself a spark within us" (p. 37). His starting point is "our creative will"—the word *creative* stressing the will's activity. This will is, however, not an isolated will. It is reflected in the will of others and, in contemplating that reflection, it consequently experiences its own incorporation in a universality, a universal will. This experience is described by Hammarskjöld as an "intuition"—a word to be observed—that leads to a "knowledge" of a power, the power which is in fact the universal will. What kind of power? No doubt a power of love; the words "a spark within us" point in that direction. His declaration, that the power is *in itself* such a spark within us, is consistent with what he has previously written about the individual will and the universal will. The universal will is the stream of all individual wills.

The correspondence between this and the main thought in Schweitzer's philosophy of life is obvious. Schweitzer's starting point was the statement: "I am life which wills to live, in the midst of life which wills to live."[1] From this he derived his programmatic watchword, Reverence for Life. Martin Lönnebo has well paraphrased Schweitzer's view: "I am one with life. I recognize myself in all the manifestations of life, because Life exists in all of them. Therefore I ought to treat all lives as if they were my own. I have reverence for my own life; therefore I also ought to have reverence for the life of others."[2] Reverence for Life means the demand to serve life. In this service the will to live, the creative will, reveals itself as a will of love, and this will of love, as it reveals itself in man, is a manifestation of the 'power,' or the 'universal will,' to live. Here is the 'ethical world-will' that is 'God.'

In his essay, "Dag Hammarskjöld and the Religions," Sven Hartman has also treated the relationship between Hammarskjöld and Schweitzer.[3] He even suggests that the entry in *Markings* from 1942 is so "Schweitzerian" that it very well could be a quotation from Schweitzer. The correspondence is indeed evident, yet there are indications that it must be Hammarskjöld's own interpretation of Schweitzer. Even in this brief statement we catch a glimpse of an attitude characteristic of Hammarskjöld. Before considering that attitude, let us first attempt to determine the kind of help Hammarskjöld received from Schweitzer's philosophy of life. Chiefly: the philosopher-physician's ethical ideal was adopted as *a universal pattern of life*. The words here italicized indicate what Hammarskjöld himself would have signified as the chief contribution of this philosophy—a *world* view denoted by Hammarskjöld, not as "faith," but as an "insight" prerequisite to faith.

A passage from 1952 gives more information concerning this universal pattern: "The stream of life through millions of years, the stream of human lives through countless centuries. Evil, death and dearth, sacrifice and love—what does 'I' mean in such a perspective? Reason tells me that I am bound to seek my own good, seek to gratify my desires, win power for myself and admiration from others. And yet I 'know'—know without knowing—that, in such a perspective, nothing could be less important. A

---

[1] Albert Schweitzer, *Out of My Life and Thought,* trans. C. T. Campion (New York: Henry Holt, 1948), p. 186.
[2] Martin Lönnebo, *Albert Schweitzers etisk-religiösa ideal* (Stockholm: Verbum, 1964), p. 166.
[3] Sven Hartman, "Dag Hammarskjöld och religionerna," *Ársskrift,* Abo Akademi (1966), pp. 31–44.

vision in which God *is*" (p. 83). Commenting on this, Professor Hartman rightly stresses its view of life's antagonisms. In life two powers oppose and fight each other: on the one hand, evil and death and dearth; and on the other hand, sacrifice and love. In confronting this universal pattern of life one sees that the seeking of one's own good, demanded by reason, is really a most negligible thing. *That* Hammarskjöld knows "without knowing" it. In using these ambiguous words he tells us that he does not mean an ordinary, rational knowledge, a point he clarifies by his reference to a vision—"a vision in which God *is*." God is the universal will of love, as it appears and acts in human sacrifice and love, in combat against evil, death, and dearth. We observe the order: sacrifice and love. The order here is not without consequence: love reveals itself primarily in the act of sacrifice. Certainly, this notion is a version of Schweitzer's philosophy of life, but Hammarskjöld's own characteristic insight informs it.

Finally, let us point to a remarkable passage from the second part of *Markings* (p.114), written when Hammarskjöld had for a long time been fully convinced that life had meaning. The statement is, he says, a self-defence against "the system-builders," although he does not disclose which system-builders he has in mind. He starts by saying that personal, individual life cannot have "a lasting intrinsic meaning," but that it can acquire a "contingent" meaning "by being fitted into and subordinated to something which 'lasts' and has a meaning in itself." This something is "Life," written with a capital letter. The way by which one finds life meaningful is the way of experience; one seeks meaning by "daring to take the leap into unconditional obedience. . . . You will find that 'in the pattern' you are liberated from the need to live 'with the herd.' You will find that, thus subordinated, your life will receive from Life all its meaning, irrespective of the conditions given you for its realization" (p.114). The words "with the herd" are not to be interpreted as proud superciliousness. No, in the lines that follow Hammarskjöld stresses that the meaningfulness of life is not dependent upon the different conditions of human life—a point of view which recurs often in *Markings*. The word *herd* simply means a life which has found no meaning. The last words in this passage accentuate that the meaning of life disappears "if anything in your personal life is allowed to slip back into the center," that is, if one falls into self-centeredness instead of living "in the pattern." No doubt, this passage—where "Life" is often written with a capital *L*—reflects Schweitzer's philosophy of life; "pattern" stands for the universal structure into which the individual life is incorporated and from which it receives meaning. As has already been pointed out, Hammarskjöld does not identify the "system-builders" against whom he defends himself. It seems probable, however, that he has in mind such "systems" as, claiming rational sanction, deny the validity of references to "experience."

When he speaks of system-builders Hammarskjöld certainly does not have Schweitzer in mind. Nevertheless, in some way even Schweitzer could be counted among the system-builders from whom Hammarskjöld dissociates himself. This is the case insofar as Schweitzer desires to build his ethical philosophy of life, his basic insight, on the foundation of "an elementary thinking" that he holds to be universally available and primary vis-à-vis different philosophical and religious conceptions. This desire does not, however, prevent him from talking of the insight as also intuition or "inner knowledge." Martin Lönnebo, in his extensive study, *Albert Schweitzer's Ethical-Religious Ideal,* says, no doubt rightly, that Schweitzer in his argumentation tries to create a synthesis of rational and intuitive arguments.[4] Here, however, Hammarskjöld is more cautious than Schweitzer. In *Markings* we find no trace of that rational "elementary thinking." As we have seen, Hammarskjöld rather believes that "reason" leads to a self-centered attitude towards life. The liberating insight is always referred to in terms of intuition. It is something that "we gain by pursuing the fleeting light in the depth of our being" (p. 37). It is to be described as a vision, or as part of the sphere of divination.

Hammarskjöld diverges from Schweitzer at the point of his view of man. Schweitzer's view of man is much more optimistic than that of Hammarskjöld. That does not mean that the outlook of the latter should be described as pessimistic. In his vision of the universal pattern of life he discovered a bright spark within us, and throughout *Markings,* in spite of all doubts and trials, he maintains this positive view. There is a rather peculiar passage from 1957 that shows how firmly he adhered to the idea of the spark. It runs: "Jesus' 'lack of moral principles.' He sat at

[4] Lönnebo, *Albert Schweitzers etisk-religiösa ideal,* p. 168.

meat with publicans and sinners, he consorted with harlots. Did he do this to obtain their votes? Or did he think that, perhaps, he could convert them by such 'appeasement'? Or was his humanity rich and deep enough to make contact, even in them, with that in human nature which is common to all men, indestructible, and upon which the future has to be built" (p.134). The intention of this statement is not—as has falsely been maintained—in all seriousness to make Jesus into a politician; it is rather an attempt to explain how Jesus could act as he did. Now, it can hardly be said that Hammarskjöld's interpretation corresponds to the Gospels' view of Jesus' action as a radical, challenging love that seeks to find neither "a spark" nor anything indestructible, but rather seeks what has been lost. But the entry is interesting because it clearly indicates Hammarskjöld's aim of maintaining in all situations his positive view of man. This view, however, is far from approximating the optimism of Schweitzer—and, indeed, that should be no surprise from a man whose self-criticism was as intent as it appears in *Markings*. To this theme we shall return in other connections.

In the foregoing we have seen that Schweitzer's philosophy of life was indisputably important to Hammarskjöld, even as we have also observed a difference between the attitudes of the two men. However, the total relationship between the two men must also be viewed from at least two other crucial points: the role of "mysticism," and the significance of Schweitzer's exegetical investigations as a "key for modern man to the world of the Gospels."

The Medieval Mystics

When Hammarskjöld in his retrospection from 1953 turns from Schweitzer to "the great medieval mystics" he begins with a *but*—a qualification of considerable importance. This doubtless means that he found something in the mystics that he did not find in Schweitzer. From what he says in *Markings* about the mystics and "the mystical experience," it is quite clear that the help he received from the mystics was in the sphere of religion. Evidently he had found Schweitzer to be greatly helpful at the point of ethics, but he found the mystics to be sources of greater assistance at the point of religion and faith.

When, in the article already mentioned, Professor Hartman tries to make precise the significance of Schweitzer for Hammarskjöld, he writes: "From a starting point in Schweitzer's thinking Hammarskjöld reached that which was fundamental in his religion: *faith as God's union with the soul.* It is true that concerning his conception of religious faith Hammarskjöld quotes Saint John of the Cross, but the road to this position led through a door opened by Schweitzer."[5] This statement, in my judgment, overestimates the influence of Schweitzer. The quotation from Saint John of the Cross, which was repeated many times, stands on its own apart from any reference by Hammarskjöld to Schweitzer. Furthermore, the important question is not whether or not Hammarskjöld's interest in "mysticism" was awakened by Albert Schweitzer; conceivably, it was, although Hammarskjöld, as we have seen, had had numerous early opportunities to become acquainted with the tradition of mysticism. The important thing is that the "mysticism" to be found in *Markings* is in fact very different from any associated with Schweitzer.

It is necessary first to observe certain features in what Schweitzer himself designated as his "mysticism." He used two expressions—mysticism as "an ethical mysticism" or as "Christ-mysticism"—whereas he rejected the idea of a "God-mysticism." Ethical mysticism. Christ-mysticism. Does one of these expressions include anything that is not to be found in the other?

"Ethical mysticism" has as its reference point the universal will as the Will-to-Love, a central idea in Schweitzer's philosophy of life. For the individual this mysticism involves primarily a demand to live and act in harmony with the universal Will-to-Love. In fact, this demand and this harmony must be self-evident, since the universal Will-to-Love is derived from the appearance of a Will-to-Love within the individuals. This accent on the will is very characteristic of Schweitzer—his philosophy of life is, indeed, a kind of philosophy of the will.

Further, what does Schweitzer mean by talking about a "Christ-mysticism?" Here, his interpretation of Paul is decisive: the proper relation to Christ means chiefly to be driven by His Spirit. In comparison with this idea any concern of Schweitzer for the "Jesus of history" is rather feeble, although he did think it possible for historical research to

[5] Sven Hartman, "Dag Hammarskjöld och religionerna," p. 34.

say something quite definite about the Jesus of history. The result of his radical investigations, however, was what Schweitzer himself described as a consistent eschatological view: the actions of Jesus were determined by the idea of the imminently approaching end and the arrival of the messianic kingdom. This interpretation Schweitzer develops in direct contrast to christological dogma on the one hand, and to the liberal or modernized picture of Jesus on the other hand. However, this eschatological interpretation, while providing a certain historical clarity, also makes Jesus a figure strange and different from modern men. To be sure, Schweitzer occasionally refers to this strangeness as a kind of engaging power: "Even if the historical Jesus has something strange about him, yet his personality, as it really is, influences us much more strongly and immediately than when he approached us in dogma and in the results attained up to the present by research."[6] But his main response to the picture of Jesus in radical eschatology is that a translation into the thought and language of modern man is now necessary. However, such a translation, according to Schweitzer, has already been performed in the letters of Paul, in the Apostle's "Christ-mysticism." Here the consistent eschatological view has been transformed into an ethical view of the kingdom of love which seeks to realize itself in this world. Schweitzer achieved this transformation by reference to the power of the Spirit of Christ: the Spirit of Christ is the spirit of love working in the hearts of men. Its demand is the service of men, and this demand, to Schweitzer, is to be heard as a demand from Christ.

Again, does "Christ-mysticism" mean something different or something more than "ethical mysticism"? In principle it does not. Yet Schweitzer would certainly have said that when eschatology is transformed into ethics Christ acts as a manifestation of the universal Will-to-Love and thus paves the way for the ethical kingdom of God in the world.

Having seen what *mysticism* meant for Schweitzer, we may ask if in fact there exists any justification for such a use of the word. I think not. Neither *ethical mysticism* nor *Christ-mysticism* displays any of the elements typical of authors who are classically described as mystics. To be sure, *mysticism* is an ambiguous term, and it is difficult to determine what is or is not typical. We shall return to that question when we have

[6] Schweitzer, *Out of My Life*, p. 70.

investigated what *mysticism* meant for Hammarskjöld. However, Schweitzer obviously interpreted *mysticism* in such a broad sense that it lost its significance. Why did he take up the word? Probably because at the time of his studies *mysticism* was a word of honor; it signified a "higher degree" of faith—even as it still does for many. Furthermore, it is very apparent that in Schweitzer's usage the word stands in sharp contrast to certain traditional views of "faith." In this connection we ought also to observe that Schweitzer had a rather critical attitude towards the medieval mysticism which meant so much to Hammarskjöld. In fact, he sharply criticizes that tradition when in *Out of My Life and Thought* he writes: "Of all the mysticism of the past it must be said that its ethical content is too slight. It puts men on the road of inwardness, but not on that of a living ethic."[7] Hammarskjöld would never have subscribed to such a statement.

It is possible to discover some traces of the influence of mysticism, even in the first part of *Markings;* the influence is most clearly seen, however, in passages written after 1953. About twenty quotations from the medieval mystics appear, most of them from Meister Eckhart and Thomas à Kempis. The definition of faith which Hammarskjöld offers at several points—that is, faith as God's union with the soul—is drawn from Saint John of the Cross. We can find also some quotations from non-Christian "mystics."

When we turn from Schweitzer's so-called mysticism to Hammarskjöld, we are immediately confronted with a striking contrast: Hammarskjöld's mysticism is a "God-mysticism"—precisely that kind of mysticism rejected by Schweitzer. To explain in detail Schweitzer's rejection would lead us too far afield; in fact, we would then be confronted with problems in Schweitzer's thinking where both difficulties and inconsistencies appear. Nevertheless, some comments must be made. According to Schweitzer, "God-mysticism" implies a thoroughly monistic view of existence. But creation—and for that reason also "the creative will"—is amoral. Therefore, if we vindicate a relation of unity or "oneness" with creation and the creative will, we are led to resignation and not to ethical

[7] Ibid., pp. 264–65.

THE MEDIEVAL MYSTICS

action. Thus it is necessary to maintain, at least in some way, a dualistic view of existence. Sometimes it seems that this notion is also used in reference to the conception of God, as well as in reference to the contradiction which exists between the amoral creative will and the universal Will-to-Love that appears in human life. No doubt, there are elements in Schweitzer's thought which demonstrate his effort to overcome this contradiction.[8] It can hardly be denied, however, that a main line in his thinking emphasizes the contrast between the creative will and the universal Will-to-Love, and that therefore God's Will-to-Love is confined to and identified with human love. Early entries in *Markings,* where Schweitzer's influence was apparent, seem to show both that Hammarskjöld interpreted him in this manner and that this interpretation became a reason for his *but* when he turned to the medieval mystics. His "God-mysticism" accords with what he found in their writings, and this necessarily means that Hammarskjöld did not look at creation and the creative will in the same critical or ambiguous manner as Schweitzer. In fact, in *Markings, creation* and *creative will* are words of the greatest honor; the will of God certainly cannot stand in contrast to the love that, together with the creative will, opposes chaos.

At this point in our investigation it is not possible to make a final estimate of the function of mysticism in *Markings.* That cannot be done before we have examined in greater detail what the book as a whole discloses about Hammarskjöld's faith. Therefore, we must here confine ourselves to some general remarks concerning the role of the medieval mystics. In his retrospection of 1953 Hammarskjöld stresses two things: first, the mystics' way of describing faith as God's union with the soul; second, their way of characterizing the life lived in union with God.

In its translation of a statement from 1954, the English version of *Markings* offers a definition of faith which Hammarskjöld drew from Saint John of the Cross: "Faith is the marriage of God and the Soul" (p. 91). This is a notable and serious mistranslation of Hammarskjöld's Swedish. Even if Saint John of the Cross did, in fact, speak at times of "a spiritual marriage with God," Hammarskjöld did not; and it seems probable that he avoided that expression consciously. The passage properly

[8] Lönnebo, *Schweitzers etisk-religiösa ideal,* pp. 232 ff.

reads: "Faith is God's union with the soul." This is perfectly in accord with Hammarskjöld's retrospection from 1953 in which he said that "faith is a state of the mind and the soul. In this sense we can understand the words of the Spanish mystic, Saint John of the Cross: 'Faith is the union of God with the soul.'"[9]

This distinction between "union" and "marriage" is important. Hammarskjöld's intention was certainly to speak of faith as an intimate relation to God, but the word *marriage* would have seemed out of place. He selected his words with the utmost care, knowing that the word *marriage* actually implied a type of medieval mysticism different from that which attracted him—a type called "bride-mysticism," chiefly represented by Saint Bernard of Clairvaux and his followers. This was a Christ-mysticism, marked by an emphasis on the feelings and described in terms of the emotional response of a bride to her bridegroom, Christ. Hammarskjöld, however, never refers to this kind of mysticism, and any use of the word *marriage* points in the wrong direction.

As we have seen from his statement of 1953, the mystics helped Hammarskjöld to see how "man should live a life of active social service in full harmony with himself as a member of the community of the spirit."[10] This statement draws our attention to two things. First, Hammarskjöld did not think that mysticism was weak at the point of ethics. On the contrary, the road from mysticism to ethical action was direct. That was *his* interpretation, many times repeated in *Markings,* of the mysticism he appreciated. Here we shall not discuss whether this view is "right" or "wrong," or if there might be something to say in favor of Schweitzer's criticisms. Our concern is simply to state how Hammarskjöld himself looked at mysticism. Second, when he says that the mystics helped him to unite the life of social action with life "as a member of the community of the spirit," he is saying something most worthy of observation. Hammarskjöld did not often talk about his spiritual life in connection with the "community of the spirit," but from the fact that this expression does appear in a statement which summarizes what was most essential to him, we must conclude that the question of the community meant more to him than we may otherwise have supposed.

---

[9] Dag Hammarskjöld, "Old Creeds in a New World," in *Servant of Peace,* ed. Wilder Foote (New York: Harper, 1962), p. 23.
[10] Ibid., p. 24.

THE MEDIEVAL MYSTICS

In Hammarskjöld's actual description of what the mystics' view of life meant to him, we meet some of the words that in *Markings* are most impressively emphasized. The help he was seeking he found "in the writings of those great medieval mystics for whom *'self-surrender'* had been the way to *self-realization,* and who in *'singleness of mind'* and *'inwardness'* had found strength to say *yes* to every demand which the needs of their neighbors made them face . . ." (italics mine). Further, the "much misused and misinterpreted word" *love* meant for the mystics "simply an overflowing of the strength with which they felt themselves filled when living in true self-oblivion. And this love found natural expressions in an unhesitant fulfillment of duty and in an unreserved acceptance of life, whatever it brought them personally of toil, suffering—or happiness." And he concludes: "I know that their discoveries about the laws of inner life and of action have not lost their significance."[11]

These statements give us valuable guidance in our effort to understand his relation—one of gratitude—to the mystics. This relationship raises many questions that we shall take into consideration at a later point in our study. Certain immediate issues nevertheless remain.

The retrospection of 1953, from which the preceding quotations have been drawn, describes his spiritual development from a Christian starting point, through skepticism and difficulties, and back to a free confession of Christian faith. This free confession Hammarskjöld himself described as a rediscovery of that which had been lost—albeit a rediscovery which was obviously also a fresh conception of the faith which very much possessed its own character. It is important to note that this is the context in which his statements about the mystics are introduced. We can legitimately conclude that he considered the mystics to be supports in his rediscovery of Christian belief.

Their language was of considerable assistance. In the foregoing we have seen how Hammarskjöld regarded certain new—and only slowly understood—insights concerning the character of religious language to be of a crucial importance. No doubt, his contact with the mystics helped him towards this discovery. In this connection another point ought also to be stressed. In the language of the mystics Hammarskjöld met a way of talking about faith that was markedly different from the ordinary, traditional religious discourse. Hans Hof, in "Christian Mysticism in Dag

[11] Ibid.

Hammarskjöld's *Markings,*" thinks that Hammarskjöld may have found in the mystics' unusual symbols for an inner experience expressions that "were or became true and adequate for him."[12] Indeed, it seems most likely that this extraordinary language fascinated him and opened doors that might otherwise have been effectively closed by worn-out expressions. This can be confirmed by the fact that many of the most familiar Christian terms—*sin, salvation, justification,* for example—scarcely ever appear in *Markings.* Yet this absence of traditional Christian terminology does not mean that the religious reality symbolized by them does not appear in *Markings.* On the contrary it is, for instance, hardly possible to talk more earnestly about "sin" than Hammarskjöld does in *Markings*—using terms that seem more meaningful to him, including those common to medieval mysticism.

There is still a point that ought to be considered, as an excursus, in this preliminary inquiry into Hammarskjöld's relation to medieval mysticism: the fact that he quotes not only Christian mystics but also those of non-Christian persuasion. We have seen that, according to Hammarskjöld himself, he looked at the medieval mystics as supports in his rediscovery of Christian faith. However, he refers also to non-Christian authors, some of them mystics. At one point Hammarskjöld quotes the Islamic mystic Rumi: "The lovers of God have no religion but God alone" (p. 103). Other quotations are drawn from old Chinese writers. One statement refers to Greek religion, another to the religion of Zoroaster. We could perhaps have expected to find some reference to Indian mysticism, so popular in recent Western literature, but nothing of that kind appears in *Markings*—a fact that, I think, may tell us something regarding Hammarskjöld's choice of citations.

What do such references mean to Hammarskjöld? Or, in a broader context and more precisely, what do they disclose concerning his attitude towards non-Christian religions? In answering this question we are certainly not confined to the statements mentioned in the preceding paragraph. Hammarskjöld has illumined this question, directly or indirectly, at many points.

[12] Hans Hof, "Kristen mystik i Dag Hammarskjölds *Vägmärken,*" *Arsbok for kristen humanism* (1964), pp. 87–95.

The question about Hammarskjöld's attitude to non-Christian religions does not actually offer any peculiar problems. His outlook can clearly be described in this way: it is neither possible nor permissible to draw any limits on God's actions in the world. God does not work only in the Christian sphere. His activity is universal, and its signs can easily be recognized everywhere in non-Christian religions. It is thus no accident that *Markings* contains quotations from non-Christian authors. On the contrary, Hammarskjöld has searched—we might say, eagerly searched—for statements that can transcend the barriers between different religions. Such an attitude was for him self-evident and consonant with the intuition that at an early point he described as "knowledge of a power which is in itself a spark within us." However, two facts contributed to the strengthening of this attitude: Hammarskjöld's intimate contacts with the mystics and his work as Secretary General. In fact, every quotation from non-Christian sources belongs to this period. And it is thus by no means surprising that he searched constantly for contacts on a level deeper than that of politics. During these years he had ample opportunity to form personal impressions of foreign cultures and religions. What he thus experienced filled him with a reverence that found voice in writings, speeches, and many letters to friends.

Two utterances regarding Hammarskjöld's general attitude to foreign cultures are worthy of citation. The first is from a letter to Bo Beskow in which he recounts his 1959 journey to East Asia. The attitude towards life which he met there was a new experience for Hammarskjöld, and that may be warrant to quote his words: "A *great* experience: how much more mature and fine the Asiatic art of living is compared to ours. Evidently you have to accept the thought that everything is an illusion, before you can master the whole scale of reality with ease, style, seriousness and happiness."[13] It need hardly be said that a view of life as "illusion" could not be accepted by one who had searched ardently for life's meaning. Still, and more profoundly, his words disclose the sympathetic openness of his attitude. The second citation is from a speech delivered in Lund in the same year, 1959. Here we meet thoughts that were characteristic of Hammarskjöld, points of view often emphasized by him. He expresses

---

[13] Bo Beskow, *Dag Hammarskjöld: Strictly Personal* (Garden City, N. Y.: Doubleday, 1969), p. 146.

his hope that men from Western civilization will go out to less favored countries in Asia and Africa with no other aim than to serve these peoples. Then he continues: "They can do it, aware of the riches of the cultural heritage which is theirs and of all that Europe stands for, but they should do it in awareness, also, that the best and soundest way to perpetuate this cultural heritage is to meet other peoples and other cultures in humble respect for the unique gifts that they, in turn, have offered and still offer to humanity.

"They should realize that it is a sign of the highest culture to be really capable of listening, learning and therefore also responding in a way which helps the less favored ones."[14]

Against this general background we now turn to a major declaration, regarding the religions of the world, that Hammarskjöld prepared for a leaflet to be given to those who visit the Meditation Room that Hammarskjöld personally planned at the United Nations in New York. The very fact that he arranged such a room of stillness and devotion is significant; but still more instructive is his explanation of the symbols used in the room. A shaft of light strikes the shimmering surface of solid rock: that is, he says, a symbol "of how the light of the spirit gives life to matter." The stone in the middle of the room, a block of iron ore, he describes in different ways: It symbolizes "the firm and permanent in a world of movement and change"; its material leads our thoughts to "the necessity of a choice between destruction and construction." In the latter words Hammarskjöld especially has in mind war and peace, but it ought to be observed that the words are also eminently crucial in *Markings*, where they refer not only to war and peace but to life as a whole. Yet, with regard to Hammarskjöld's view of the world's religions, the following explanation of the stone in the Meditation Room is decisive: "We may see it as an altar, empty not because there is no God, not because it is an altar to an unknown God, but because it is dedicated to the God whom man worships under many names and in many forms."[15] There is, this statement affirms, something common to all religions in spite of

---

[14] Dag Hammarskjöld, "Asia, Africa and the West," in *Servant of Peace* (see n. 9 above), p. 217.
[15] Dag Hammarskjöld, "A Room of Quiet," in *Servant of Peace* (see n. 9 above), p. 160.

all differences. And we must not overlook that he describes the stone as an altar. Altar and sacrifice, from of old and in countless religions, belong together; certainly they did for Hammarskjöld—*sacrifice* is a cardinal word in *Markings*.

Now let us look at three passages in *Markings*. Two, drawn from Chinese texts, are closely related to each other; they are separated, or joined, by a short reference to Meister Eckhart. The first, Hammarskjöld introduces with the words, "The ultimate experience is *one*," meaning: one thing and only one, or, as in the English translation, "the same for all." The text then runs: "Only the most absolute sincerity under heaven can bring the inborn talent to the full and empty the chalice of the nature. He who can totally sweep clean the chalice of himself can carry the inborn nature of others to its fulfillment . . . this clarifying activity has no limit, it neither stops nor stays . . . it stands in the emptiness above with the sun, seeing and judging, interminable in space and time, searching, enduring . . . unseen it causes harmony; unmoving it transforms; unmoved it perfects" (p. 117). In an annotation Hammarskjöld adds, "*Tsze Sze,* not Eckhart," obviously thinking that the text is so much in harmony with Eckhart that confusion could be possible. Further, this brief annotation can be seen as an expression of Hammarskjöld's own astonishment at discovering a resemblance between the Chinese text and Eckhart. Hammarskjöld's preliminary words must thus mean that the ultimate experience is one and the same, as far as it is a God-experience, an experience of the God who always is one and the same. This view is congruent with his words about the "altar" in the Meditation Room, that God is worshiped in many forms. The Chinese text indicates that in Hammarskjöld's view we can sometimes find a correspondence between Christian and non-Christian "forms," between their respective expressions of the ultimate experience. Such a correspondence confirms the unity of the ultimate God-experience.

Following the first Chinese text there is a brief passage which leads to the second Chinese text. On occasion, as here, successive passages demonstrate a continuity of thought. In this case there are difficulties—compounded by infelicities in the English translation. The text runs: "*Semina motuum.* In us the creative power [English: the creative instinct] became will. In order to grow beautifully like a tree, we have to attain that rest in the unity [English: a peaceful self-unity] in which the creative will is retransformed into instinct. —Eckhart's 'habitual will'" (p.117*). When we compare this text with similar texts in *Markings,* there can be no doubt that "creative power" and "unity" have reference to God. Certainly, Hammarskjöld *can* talk about a "rest at the center of our being" (p.148), but such a rest exists only in that unity which is God. It is on this basis that the line of thought continues in the following Chinese text where, in a most audacious way, Hammarskjöld tries to find an analogue between the Christian Trinity and an ethical Confucian "trinity." We read: "'—looking straight into one's own heart—(as we can do in the mirror-image of the Father)—watching with affection the way people grow—(as in imitation of the Son)—coming to rest in perfect equity' (as in the fellowship of the Spirit). The ultimate experience corresponds to our ethical experience. Even the Way of the Confucian world has its 'trinity'" (p.117*).

The comparison of these two "trinities" discloses Hammarskjöld's eagerness to find relations regarding the ethical attitude of the two partners. It seems farfetched to speak here about two "trinities." However, the quotation marks around the word *trinity* show that Hammarskjöld himself is quite conscious of the relative significance of the word. His main intention is simply to demonstrate the similarity of his own ethical reactions and those found in the Chinese text. Why, then, does he use the expression *trinity?* The word is not unknown in *Markings.* It appears sometimes directly, sometimes indirectly, and Hammarskjöld is able to speak of his reactions to the Trinity very much in the same way as in the comparison now discussed. In an entry written at the beginning of 1956, he says: *"Before* Thee, Father, / In righteousness and humility, / *With* Thee, Brother, / In faithfulness and courage, / *In* Thee, Spirit, / In stillness" (p.109). These reactions and those in his comments on the Chinese text can be described as, first, self-examination before the Father; second, faithfulness, imitation, service in love, in communion with the Son or the Brother (as usually he prefers to say); and finally, stillness in fellowship with the Spirit. The important thing is that he finds a relationship between these and his reactions to the Chinese text. That the "trinity" is allowed to accompany the latter statement is of minor importance.

Finally, we shall look at an important passage from Good Friday 1956.

"The third hour. And the ninth. That is *now*. And *now*—that *is* now! 'Jesus will be in agony even to the end of the world. We must not sleep during that time.' (Pascal.) We must not— And for the watcher is the far-off present—also present in his contact with mankind among whom, at every moment, Jesus dies in someone who has followed the trail marks of the inner road to the end: love and patience, / righteousness and humility, / faithfulness and courage, / stillness" (p.111*).

We shall later return to these words, with their strong accent on simultaneousness and coexistence with the Crucified. Here we shall consider their reference to mankind as a whole. The watcher finds the far-off present in immediate contact with mankind; here "Jesus dies in someone who has followed the trail marks" to the end. In interpreting this text we first must notice that Hammarskjöld uses symbolic language in speaking of Jesus as "dying" in others. The symbol points to a service that sacrifices itself even unto death. This symbol explains for the "watcher," Hammarskjöld, what an imitation of the Crucified must mean; the final watchwords point to the way of following the marks of the "inner road." But for *this* watcher it is not possible to meditate in the presence of the Crucified or to experience the presence of the far-off without being brought into contact with humanity as a whole. The symbol of the dying Jesus can be applied whenever a human being sacrifices himself without restrictions. Here Hammarskjöld writes of a sacrifice that has always been at the center of Christian thinking, and yet, precisely here do his thoughts transcend all boundaries. It is hardly possible to speak more effectively about the universality of the divine activity.

Our interpretation of these passages is also an interpretation of the words about the "altar" in the Meditation Room. It should now be clear why the stone, as Hammarskjöld said, "may be seen as an altar." Here is deep respect for what can be found in all the religions of the world.

Finally, two remarks concerning this attitude of Hammarskjöld's. First, it is obviously allied spiritually to Schweitzer's attitude. However, we must point out that as early as his student years at Uppsala Hammarskjöld may very well have found the same positive attitude towards the non-Christian religions in the writings of Nathan Söderblom, who possessed a deep respect for all authentic piety. Further, there is no doubt that Hammarskjöld's contacts with the medieval mystics were influential —not least his contact with the most speculative of these mystics, Meister

Eckhart. Hammarskjöld's formula, that the ultimate experience is one and the same, hardly could have been written apart from Eckhart's influence. It is significant that the passage where this statement appears and where, then, Hammarskjöld quotes a Chinese text, ends with a note that Tsze Sze, not Eckhart, is the author. Second, we have no evidence that Hammarskjöld adopted a syncretistic view towards religion. He quoted non-Christian authors, not to seek help from their writings, but because he found in them signs of God's universal activity. That meant much to him not only as a matter of principle but also in view of his worldwide service as Secretary General of the United Nations.

Meditations before the Gospels' Picture of Jesus

Markings contains about fifty quotations from the Bible, not to mention many allusions to biblical sources. Half of the quotations are drawn from the Psalter, which in spite of the fact that Hammarskjöld wrote in Swedish is invariably cited in English according to the usage of the Anglican Psalter. Most of the other biblical quotations are from the Gospels, with almost nothing from the Epistles; there are also citations from Genesis, Isaiah, and the Book of Revelation.

Looking at Hammarskjöld in relation to the Gospels, we once more meet the name of Albert Schweitzer. We have seen that the influence of Schweitzer's philosophy was considerable, at least during Hammarskjöld's period of crisis. Yet a case may also be made for claiming that Schweitzer's chief influence on Hammarskjöld was rather related to his critical investigations of the Gospels, as presented in *The Quest of the Historical Jesus* (1906).[16] In these researches Hammarskjöld found "a key for modern man to the world of the Gospels."

It is, I think, well within possibility to fix exactly what Hammarskjöld meant by the "key." If we take into consideration only Schweitzer's exegetical theories, we see his influence as rather limited. In *Markings* we do not find any trace of his main idea, his strong emphasis on "consistent eschatology," to use the phrase which has become a catchword.

---

[16] Albert Schweitzer, *The Quest of the Historical Jesus: A Critical Study of Its Progress from Reimarus to Wrede,* trans. W. Montgomery (New York: Macmillan, 1961).

Nor do we find signs of Schweitzer's theory that Jesus died with the intention of accelerating the arrival of the messianic kingdom and reducing the torments before its coming. There was only *one* point which was important to Hammarskjöld: the critical scholarship which reveals Jesus to be a human being, living and acting in a quite distinct historical situation. He could, of course, have found this same view in the work of many other scholars; for him, however, Schweitzer was the man with the "key," and it was his presentation of the Gospels' picture of Jesus which was for Hammarskjöld a fact of utmost weight. Therefore—and only therefore—he considered Schweitzer's "key" a great and indispensable gift. He had, no doubt, felt that traditional Christology concealed this picture of Jesus' "true humanity." To be sure, the old christological dogma spoke not only of Jesus' divinity but also of his humanity, but theology had nevertheless so organized its discussion of the person of Jesus that his humanity hardly ever appeared in a concrete and realistic manner. For Hammarskjöld this undisguised picture of a human Jesus, as presented by Schweitzer, called forth a new set of relationships. The view of Jesus as a divine being in human dress had kept Hammarskjöld at a distance; now he approached Jesus as a brother in the human family. The human Jesus—and this was not Hammarskjöld's only or last view of Jesus; it was the introductory and decisive view—was the Gospel's Jesus, the Brother whom he followed "step by step" through the years.

From this starting point let us go on to examine the two passages from *Markings,* written before 1953, which have a direct relation to Jesus. The first, from 1940, is very short. "O Caesarea Philippi: to accept condemnation of the Way as its fulfillment and presupposition, to accept this both when it is chosen and when it is realized" (p. 50*). Upon the appearance of *Markings* this passage was horribly misunderstood by one Swedish reviewer, who thought that it implied that Hammarskjöld had seen himself as a new Messiah. In the text there is of course not the slightest glimpse of such an absurd idea. When we read the passage in its context and in connection with the reference to Caesarea Philippi in Mark 8, the meaning of the exclamation "O Caesarea Philippi" becomes quite clear.

In the section preceding this exclamation we meet thoughts which frequently appeared during this period of Hammarskjöld's life. He speaks candidly of the emptiness and self-disgust that were his companions in the work he performed. He doubts the importance of his task, and sees himself as "perhaps ... slowly nearing the point where he will feel grateful when he is not criticized, but he is still a very long way from accepting criticism when he is" (p. 50). He has asked for burdens to carry, but he howls when they are placed on his shoulders. "Did you believe in the anonymity of sacrifice? The sacrificial act and the sacrificial victim are opposites, and to be judged as such" (p. 36). This difficult Swedish text could be literally rendered: "The sacrifice of the sacrificial act is to be judged as its antithesis"—meaning: the sacrifice will not be appreciated but criticized and condemned; it belongs to the sacrifice to accept the condemnation. Then follows the eloquent cry beginning "O Caesarea Philippi."

It is sufficient to recall, as further explication, that in Mark 8 Peter confesses his faith—"You are the Christ"—and Jesus responds by speaking of approaching suffering and sacrifice. Jesus, subsequently, rebukes Peter for trying to persuade him to escape that suffering and sacrifice: "If any man would come after me, let him deny himself and take up his cross and follow me."

It is quite clear that this crucial section of *Markings* refers primarily to the behavior of Jesus: *he* chooses the way of sacrifice without hesitation, quite aware that it must lead to condemnation. And this same view of Jesus' action returns several times in *Markings*. Hammarskjöld sees Jesus in contrast to his own faltering position as one who shrinks from "accepting criticism." Inquiries which had already entered his mind now became actualized in a new light; he seems to have heard the voice of Jesus as a severe accusation directed to himself. Of course, it can be said that this challenge includes an invitation to discipleship, but that is a question not yet in focus for Hammarskjöld. The exclamation "O Caesarea Philippi" clearly refers to Jesus and his challenge.

The second statement concerning Jesus from this period before 1953 is the longest passage in *Markings* and, certainly, one of its most important. It is clearly fundamental to an understanding of Hammarskjöld's view both of the Gospels' picture of Jesus and of his own relation to him. Therefore, it is necessary carefully to ponder this marking (pp. 72–3). With consummate artistry Hammarskjöld paints a vivid and most suggestive picture of the last evening of Jesus' life. The first words are impressive: "A young man, adamant in his commitment to life" (English text: his committed life). Adamant—here is no trace of the sentimentality that so often has distorted and falsified the image of Jesus. Hammarskjöld stresses his loneliness—"alone as he confronted his final destiny." "He had assented to a possibility in his being. . . . If God required anything of him, he would not fail." "Only recently" had Jesus begun to see that the "road of possibility might lead to the Cross." (In the word *recently* the influence of Schweitzer's interpretation may be traced.) "He knew, though, that he had to follow it, still uncertain as to whether he was indeed 'the one who shall bring it to pass,' but certain that the answer could only be learned by following the road to the end. The end *might* be a death without significance—as well as being the end of the road of possibility" (p. 72).

In the framework of this picture Hammarskjöld raises two questions. The first, "Is the hero of this immortal, brutally simple drama in truth 'the Lamb of God that taketh away the sins of the world'? Absolutely faithful to a divined possibility—in that sense the Son of God, in that sense the sacrificial Lamb, in that sense the Redeemer. A young man, adamant in his commitment, who walks the road of possibility to the end without self-pity or demand for sympathy, fulfilling the destiny he has chosen—even sacrificing affection and fellowship when the others are unready to follow him—into a new fellowship" (pp. 72-3).

Hammarskjöld had presented a fresh and very human picture of Jesus, and now it was necessary to set this picture in contrast to the biblical message about Christ and the traditional church-inspired doctrines. It is interesting to see how Hammarskjöld treats this question—he is neither affirmative nor negative. Nevertheless, even though his attitude can best be described as one of tentative expectancy, he offers some suggestions which intimate that he could find the biblical description of Jesus as Son of God, Lamb of God, Redeemer, meaningful. Hammarskjöld's decisive perspective is absolute faithfulness to "a divined possibility"; self-sacrifice, consequently, is affirmed as the only conceivable way to realize this possibility. *Sacrifice* is thus the key word, and in times to come Hammarskjöld's thoughts were more and more to become engaged with the meaning of this word—not least, the notion of sacrifice as an action of divine love.

If this first question was a question that he raised out of necessity, the second had a purely personal character. It was, indeed, from the depths of his heart. "Assenting to his possibility—why? Does he sacrifice himself for others, *yet for his own sake*—in megalomania? Or does he realize himself for the sake of others? The difference is that between a monster and a man. 'A new commandment I give unto you: that ye love one another'" (p. 73). Most probably, Hammarskjöld affirmed the second alternative. He found the consummate sacrifice "for the sake of others" to be an example worthy of emulation. He heard the exhortation to follow this brother, and he assented in obedience to "the new commandment." Here was a fragment of the yes which was growing during the years of his spiritual crisis.

Hammarskjöld ends this long passage with two reflections, one about Jesus and one about himself. The first speaks of Jesus' entrance into Jerusalem and the shouts of Hosanna—"shouts which opened up other possibilities than the one he had chosen." As we already have seen, this account is also echoed in another reflection where, after his election as Secretary General, Hammarskjöld reminds himself that possible success must not conceal the fact that the way was to be one of sacrifice and cross.

The second reflection, a very personal meditation, ends with the following words: "—in the end, the vista of future loneliness only allows a choice between two alternatives: either to despair in desolation, or to stake so high on the 'possibility' that one acquires the right to life in a communion beyond the individual. But doesn't choosing the second call for the kind of faith which moves mountains?" (p. 73*). The passage ends with this question—unanswered. We can make the following judgment: to follow the Brother in obedience to the new commandment is not the same as to come to faith and to enter a new fellowship which is "beyond the individual." Hammarskjöld's yes is growing, but it is not yet a complete yes.

Our survey of this entry in Hammarskjöld's diary has shown that two things are fundamental to his estimate of Jesus' sacrifice. First, it must have been a sacrifice only for others with no admixture of self-centeredness, with no trace of "megalomania." Second, when Jesus chose the way of sacrifice his choice was—must have been—a risk; he could have had no certainty as to the results of the choice. His action must—if I may say so—have had an experimental character. Thus if Jesus himself had possessed a self-evident certainty that death on the cross would be only a transition to resurrection, then the sacrifice would have lost its meaning. Hammarskjöld as a matter of fact always maintained these convictions concerning the significance of Jesus' sacrificial action. This is demonstrated in a writing of 1957 where he deals with the meaning of sacrifice. Here he talks about faith as upholding sacrifice—a faithfulness (the proper translation) "alone among enemies and skeptics," a faithfulness "in spite of the humiliation," a faithfulness "without any hope of compensation other than he can find in a faith which reality seems so thoroughly to refute." Then he continues: "Would the action of sacrifice [English translation: the Crucifixion] have had any sublimity or meaning if the offering [English translation: Jesus] had seen himself crowned with the halo of martyrdom? What we have added was not there for him. And we must forget all about it if we are to hear his commands (p. 130*). The English translation expresses clearly what Hammarskjöld had in mind. "What we have added"—that is, the reference to the resurrection "on the third day" which in each of the synoptic Gospels follows Jesus' own forecast of his sufferings and death must, according to Hammarskjöld, have been added. This was an idea the certainty of which was "not there for Him."

It is no wonder that Hammarskjöld's picture of Jesus has attracted much attention and been subjected to different evaluations. Two of these are worthy of reference. Henry Pitney Van Dusen says: "A rigid orthodoxy might brand this reading of Jesus' consciousness as he confronted his end heretical; it explicitly challenges the tradition that he foresaw a vindication in Resurrection and Exaltation. Can we doubt that Hammarskjöld gives the historically correct interpretation? Moreover, it perfectly reflects the fashion in which he had found in Jesus his Guide for life."[17]

A Swedish scholar in the area of psychology of religion, Hjalmar Sundén, has written a study concerning Hammarskjöld's meditations on Christ which is from many points of view most valuable.[18] However, he

---

[17] Henry Pitney Van Dusen, *Dag Hammarskjöld: The Statesman and His Faith* (New York: Harper, 1967), p. 197.
[18] Hjalmar Sundén, *Kristusmeditationer i Dag Hammarskjölds Vägmärken* (Stockholm: Verbum, 1966), pp. 49, 72.

very often operates with terms such as "heterodox," "undogmatic," or "non-Lutheran," and then attempts to demonstrate how Hammarskjöld's attitude changed during the years. Sundén asserts that *Markings* reveals a shift from an early position of heterodoxy to, in later years, an acceptance of "the Christian dogma" and "the doctrine of *satisfactio vicaria*." We shall at a later point scrutinize the accuracy of this assertion.

It must be questioned whether the traditional designations of Christian theology are relevant and helpful in an analysis of *Markings*. What do the words *orthodox* and *heterodox* mean? What qualifies a theology as orthodox? In the different "churches" there are different kinds of orthodoxy. In the history of "Lutheran" theology, for example, a specific era in history has been called the period of orthodoxy. It certainly would be meaningless to examine *Markings* according to the standards of that "orthodoxy." Will not slogans of this kind lead our attention away from what the document really contains? We must bear in mind that words such as *orthodox* and *heterodox* are expressions charged with emotion: for some they are designations of honor; for others, designations of reproach.

However, quite apart from these considerations, there is another question that must certainly be raised. How correct was Hammarskjöld's interpretation of the biblical texts? Obviously, Hammarskjöld could not have written as he did if he had not been aware of the historico-critical study of the Bible. This study must have convinced him that the sayings ascribed to Jesus in the Gospels are not always to be considered authentic. In the first three Gospels, the Synoptics, we meet the same pattern: Jesus' prediction of his approaching death is consistently accompanied by a prediction of the resurrection. Whether or not such a pattern might in some shape have been familiar to Jesus himself must, of course, be discussed, although it is not possible to reach a final conclusion here. Still, it is not this source-critical question, as such, that has the decisive weight for Hammarskjöld. The important thing for him is the *risk* involved in Jesus' choice: "the end *might* be a death without significance." The thought of a resurrection may have been in his mind; that does not necessarily eliminate the risk. The risk, however, must have been a constituent element in the choice; if not, the sacrifice would have been fictitious and Jesus would have been either a megalomaniacal monster or not a true human being. In fact, if we eliminate the risk from Jesus' conscience, then as Hammarskjöld says, we are adding something that "was not there for Him." We can, I think, agree with Van Dusen in asking if there is any doubt that Hammarskjöld gives the historically correct interpretation. Indeed, does not Jesus' prayer in Gethsemane confirm this interpretation? And the cry from the cross: "My God, my God, why hast Thou forsaken me?" The fact that Matthew and Mark recorded only these words from the cross might not mean that they knew no others; but certainly it means that these words were decisive for them. Hammarskjöld's view is, in fact, quite in harmony with the primitive Christian confession of the true humanity of Christ. If "rigid orthodoxy" holds a different opinion we must conclude that—as has so often been the case—that orthodoxy has itself adopted the docetic heresy whereby the genuine humanity of Jesus is concealed and distorted.

Chapter Four

YES TO GOD

Two Definitions of Faith

Dag Hammarskjöld's *yes* appeared for the first time at New Year's, 1953. His entry for that day begins with the same quotation from a well-known Swedish hymn that he had used in earlier New Year's entries and that he would use again at the start of 1954 and 1957. The quotation runs: "Night is drawing nigh." Van Dusen[1] is quite right in pointing out that this hymn is not—as the English translation of *Markings* seems to suggest—an ordinary hymn for the evening; it is rather a meditation on the transience of life:

> How vain the worlding's pomp and show,
> How brief his joys and pleasures!
> The night approaches now, and lo!
> We leave all earthly treasures.

After citing this familiar hymn, Hammarskjöld continues: "For all that has been—Thanks! To all that shall be—Yes!" (p. 87). Here begins a new melody in *Markings*. In the past years the dominant tunes had been those of struggle and despair, in spite of the presence of some intimations of brightness. Hammarskjöld had been led to the frontier of the unheard-of, but only to the frontier. Now the situation is different. His thanks for the past and his yes to that which is to come mean that he has passed the frontier and that a new time has arrived. In 1954 Hammarskjöld comments on the words with which he entered 1953. After an affirmation of his newly won freedom he writes: "Thanks to those who

---

[1] Henry Pitney Van Dusen, *Dag Hammarskjöld: The Statesman and His Faith* (New York: Harper, 1967), p. 71.

have taught me this. Thanks to the days which have taught me this." He continues, "Then I saw that the wall had never been there, that the 'unheard-of' is here and this, not something and somewhere else, that the 'offering' is here and now, always and everywhere—'surrendered' *to be* what, in me, God gives of Himself to Himself" (pp. 90–1).

Hammarskjöld repeats this *yes* often. It is a yes to God but also to oneself, to life and to destiny. In summary: "Yes to God: yes to destiny and yes to yourself" (p. 135*). *Yes to God* is decisive, and it includes the other two elements.

Yes to God means faith in God. Hammarskjöld describes faith in many ways; two of these provide definitions. One, from Saint John of the Cross: "Faith is God's union with the soul." The other: faith, or the "unheard-of," is "to be in the hands of God" or "under the hands of God." Both "definitions" are repeated several times in *Markings*.

It is worth observing that Hammarskjöld found certain words of one of the mystics relevant when he tried to explain what faith meant to him. This indicates his indebtedness to the mystics precisely at the time when his growing and hidden yes was being transformed into an open one. The other definition is drawn directly from both the Old and the New Testaments, where "in the hands of God" and related expressions often appear. In *Markings* this second formula appears twice, shortly after the reference to faith as union with God. When Hammarskjöld here speaks of faith in terms of the hands of God, it seems probable that he has the Psalter especially in mind—the biblical book he most frequently quotes. After two statements about being in God's hand, he quotes Psalm 139: "If I take the wings of the morning and remain in the uttermost parts of the sea; / even there also shall thy hand lead me" (p. 94). Two definitions of faith: one from the mystics, one from the Bible. By no means does this imply that the first definition has no roots in the Bible, and still less that Hammarskjöld saw that definition as unbiblical. In fact, he could have found similar expressions in Paul and John; he made, however, almost no direct references to the epistles.

In memoirs where an author records his sudden conversion we sometimes find a more or less penetrating description of what happened at a precise moment—as, for example, Augustine's celebrated narrative in the *Confessiones*. As we have seen, Hammarskjöld's spiritual development was quite different—his yes grew only gradually. For that reason, we cannot expect to find a detailed description of the manner in which his experience took shape. Nevertheless, *Markings* gives us at least some hints. Certain oft-repeated words, typically enough drawn from the vocabulary of the medieval mystics, are significant: *stillness* and *silence*. In stillness God meets the soul. In this connection it is interesting to observe that Hammarskjöld often combines "stillness" with "Spirit": *"In* Thee, Spirit, / In stillness" (p.109): the Spirit of God is present in stillness. And we ought especially to note the passage in which for the first time Hammarskjöld speaks of faith as God's union (not marriage) with the soul (p. 91*). Immediately he asserts, in harmony with his view of the nature of religious language, that "Faith *is*: it cannot, therefore, be comprehended, far less identified with the formulae in which we paraphrase what is" (p. 91*). All descriptions are inadequate—but that does not reduce the significance of that which *is,* of faith as a reality. He expands on this by again quoting Saint John of the Cross, and now in Spanish: "—'en una noche oscura.' The Dark Night of the Soul—so dark that we may not even look for faith. The night in Gethsemane when the last friends left you have fallen asleep, all the others are seeking your downfall, and *God is silent,* as the union is consummated" (p. 91*).

These words can be interpreted as a testimony to Hammarskjöld's experience. He speaks not only of stillness but also of darkness, *noche oscura.* He remembers the picture of Jesus as once he painted it; his thoughts turn to Gethsemane. In spite of all, he believes, Jesus had not been forsaken—even if God was silent. On the contrary: what really happened was the consummation of the union, a consummation of faith. In Gethsemane, we must conclude, Hammarskjöld found a parallel to his own experience. Thus, the passage sets forth three things. First, it describes an experience undergone in the darkest night and in utter loneliness, in the time of his own deepest struggle. Second, it asserts that this experience was not initiated by any activity of his own, not even by his search for faith. Third, and therefore, the experience is a mystery—which is accentuated by the description of the silent God. The quality of mystery could hardly be more emphatically stressed.

En una noche oscura—these words are, no doubt, significant in respect to the manner in which for Hammarskjöld "God's union with the soul" came into existence. And with these words we must be satisfied. Hammarskjöld neither would nor could say more about the mystery, but, in contrast, he has much to say concerning the meaning of this union. Let us now turn to an investigation of the two definitions of faith: "union with God" and "being in the hands of God." We have seen that the two expressions have different origins, but they do not have dissimilar meanings; they are intimately connected with each other. They describe the same God-relationship: union with God means to be in the hands of God; to be in the hands of God means to be in union with him. Hammarskjöld sees faith as a relationship between God and man. Now, in a relationship two partners act, and thus our questions become: What was the role of God? And what was the role of Hammarskjöld himself?

Faith is God's union with the soul. This statement includes three important perspectives: the relation to God is a relation of faith; the word *union* characterizes the quality of the faith; the word *God's,* in possessive form, stresses the primary activity of God in this relationship.

Faith is the principal word for man's relation to God. All of man's contacts with God are contacts in and through faith. Apart from faith there is no possibility for contact with God; he cannot be reached by the simple use of man's natural faculties—as, for example, his powers of reason. This means that all statements about God are at the same time statements about faith. Speculative statements about him apart from faith are only fanciful.

That Hammarskjöld would consider *union* the word most suited for describing the quality of faith can easily be understood. We have seen that even early in *Markings* he was most aware that the question of faith was a very personal, intimate question, one essentially related to all of life. Consequently, his statements about faith were polemically directed against any idea that faith was primarily assent to doctrines. In *union* he found a word which firmly emphasized the existential character of faith.

This existential quality of faith as man's relation to God was often expressed by Hammarskjöld in formulas such as "God in me." After his first *yes* one of the succeeding writings runs: "Not I, but God in me" (p. 87). And shortly thereafter we read: "I am the vessel. The draught is God's. And God is the thirsty one" (p. 88). The formula "God in me" appears frequently in *Markings,* but Hammarskjöld can also say about himself, "you in God." These expressions appear together in the following passage from 1958: "In the faith which is 'God's union with the soul,' you are *one* in God, and God is wholly in you, just as, for you, He is wholly in all you meet" (p.139*). The perspective "you in God" appears quite naturally, furthermore, whenever faith is described as being in God's hands.

On Christmas Day 1956 Hammarskjöld wrote about union with God, making reference to Meister Eckhart's words *"Von der ewigen Geburt"*: "'Of the Eternal Birth'—to me, this now says everything there is to be said about what I have learned and have still to learn" (p. 124). Such words must be interpreted in the context of Hammarskjöld's formula, "God in me." Although written at Christmas, the statement ought not to be interpreted as "Christ-mysticism." The theme is God and the soul. The passage which immediately precedes this, likewise a quotation from Eckhart, also dwells on this theme: the man who has only God in view "must learn to pierce the veil of things and comprehend God *within them.*" That God is "born" in the soul means that he is revealing himself and that in the power of his will he unites the soul with himself. That is the eternal birth: a birth that belongs not only to time but to eternity. Hammarskjöld concludes by quoting Eckhart concerning the preconditions of this birth-experience. Here again we find the accent upon stillness and silence: "The soul that would experience this birth must detach herself from all outward things: within herself completely at one with herself . . . . You must have an exalted mind and a *burning* heart in which, nevertheless, reign silence and stillness."

There exists, as is well known, a God-mysticism in which union with God becomes an identity with God. Hammarskjöld's "union with God" does not belong to this mysticism. He clearly and strongly emphasizes the distance between God and man. Indications of this distance are to be found everywhere in Hammarskjöld's descriptions of his "negotiations" with God: in the way in which God is addressed, in prayers, in his self-examination before God, in all that is said about the activity of God. In this union with God, He is the giver; but at the same time He places demands on those with whom He is united.

God can be addressed with the intimate pronoun, *Thou,* and he can also be described with the anonymous word, the *Other.* In both cases distance is stressed. The Thou is beyond us: "Thou who art over us" (p. 93). Union means to be in or under God's hand; in the passage just cited Hammarskjöld also wrote: "For I am under Thy hand, / And in Thee is all power and goodness."

The same elements are at play in the prayers which appear frequently in *Markings,* some few in the first part, most after the appearance of Hammarskjöld's *yes.* To the earlier prayers he gave this form, "Pray that your loneliness may spur you into finding something to live for, great enough to die for" (p. 85). Here he exhorts himself to pray, but in the later period he does not need such an exhortation, for his prayers are then addressed directly to God. He turns to God with supplications for his soul and for his work—as, for example, in a short prayer built around the Our Father:

> Hallowed be Thy name,
> *not mine,*
> Thy kingdom come,
> *not mine,*
> Thy will be done,
> *not mine,*
> Give us peace with Thee
> Peace with men
> Peace with ourselves,
> And free us from all fear. (p. 123.)

All the prayers bear clear witness to the distance between God and man, but they also affirm the nearness of God. The passages of self-examination, so abundant in *Markings,* portray the same scrutiny of God. The affirmation of God and indeed even union with God do not stop this scrutiny. On the contrary: "The experience of religious reality . . . forces the 'Night side' out into the light" (p. 128). In all of the book's meditations, which often assume the character of prayer, there is a vivid consciousness of the scrutinizing eye of God: "*Before* Thee, Father, / In righteousness and humility" (p. 109).

The activity of God, as presented in *Markings,* is described chiefly in terms of the distance between God and man. One of Hammarskjöld's main themes is the distinction between the Creator and creation. God, as creator, is always creating. On Christmas Day 1955 he quotes Thomas à Kempis' description of this distinction: "But when in this way they taste God, be it in Himself or in His works, they recognize at the same time that there is an infinite distance between the creature and the Creator, time and eternity" (p. 105).

According to both of Hammarskjöld's definitions of faith, God is seen as the Giver but at the same time as One who inevitably makes demands. Union with God, the "unheard-of," is a gift of God; it is *"to be* what, in me, God gives of Himself to Himself" (p. 91). In this connection a quotation from Eckhart ought to be noted: "There is a contingent and non-essential will: and there is, providential and creative, an habitual will. God has never given Himself, and never will, to a will alien to His own: where He finds His will, He gives Himself" (p.111). This is a statement concerning the possibility of and prerequisites for receiving that gift of God which is no less than the gift of Himself. Obviously, the implication is not that the condition is some meritorious performance of man. What God seeks is "His own will." It would not be wrong here to think of "the spark within us," an expression we have met at an earlier stage in our study. This spark has its origin in God and is in itself a gift of God. However, union with God is not realized in that spark; it is being realized, here and now, through the action of God's providential and creative will, which is in process of becoming a habitual will within us. Union with God, thus realized, includes "forgiveness." This inclusion emphasizes simultaneously the distance from God and the fullness of union with him: "In the presence of God, nothing stands between Him and us—we *are* forgiven. But we *cannot* feel His presence if anything is allowed to stand between ourselves and others" (p. 110). I will later return to the question of forgiveness, an issue which was doubtless a great problem for Hammarskjöld.

In 1957 Hammarskjöld writes most feelingly about the activity of God. He first cites Eckhart to the effect that the most wonderful thing that can happen in this life "is that you should be silent and let God work and speak." Then he elaborates: "Long ago, you gripped me, Slinger. *Now* into Thy storm. *Now* towards Thy target" (p.134*). It could hardly be said more clearly that union with God, being in his hands, is a result of

God's prior action. Still, not even here does Hammarskjöld speak only about God as a giver; he is at the same time a God who presents demands: there are works to be performed in his service.

God is the one who gives orders. Union with God is not possible without obedience to these orders. They are given "in secret"—we could also say that they are given when the soul listens, in stillness, to the voice of God. What God then requires is service. Service of God—yes, of course. But this service can be performed only as service towards men. But, as will become apparent, God's orders do not prescribe in detail what is or is not to be done. What God claims, from first to last, is surrender of the self. Then the obedient man must himself decide how to act in different situations—always at his own risk. "Forward! Thy orders are given in secret. May I always hear them—and obey. Forward! Whatever distance I have covered, it does not give me the right to halt. Forward! It is the attention given to the last steps before the summit which decides the value of all that went before" (p.125).

Hitherto we have seen the stress Hammarskjöld lays upon the distance between God and man and the way in which the union with God is realized, as a gift, through the action of God. Yet this does not mean that man is to be passive. In the history of Christian thought we sometimes discover a reluctance to speak about the activity of man in respect to God —owing to a potential identification of man with merit. But the notion of merit is unfamiliar and alien to Hammarskjöld, and hence he is able to speak as frankly as the New Testament itself about the activity of man.

Man's activity makes its first appearance when the answer *yes* is given to God. This is faith when seen from the side of man. Thus man receives the gift of God: he is in the hands of God, in union with him. Hammarskjöld speaks often about the quality and the meaning of this action as seen from the perspective of man. But all that he says can be summed up in two important words: *self-surrender* and *self-realization*. The first word describes the action negatively; the second, positively. These two attitudes are intimately connected with each other—in the yes to God. This *yes* means saying no to the self, self-surrender; but it means at the same time saying yes to yourself, self-realization. On the way of self-surrender there is, paradoxically, self-realization—because self-surrender means surrender to God.

There are few words so often repeated in the second part of *Markings* as the word *surrender* and its related terms. That Hammarskjöld considered *surrender* to be the primary word is evidenced by the fact that in the original Swedish text he on occasion uses the English word *surrender*. In his desire to paint the attitude of surrender in various colors he also makes use of other, more or less equivalent, modes of speech: "In God I am nothing" (p. 88); "forget yourself completely" (p. 131); "those who have lost themselves in God" (p. 96*; here, the English translation, "those who have forgotten themselves," is incorrect). Hammarskjöld also writes of *self-effacement,* an interesting term because of Hammarskjöld's own ambiguous attitude towards it. This ambiguity is more apparent in the Swedish text than in the English translation, where "effacement" sometimes has been replaced by "self-forgetfulness" or "dying-unto-self" (the second expression certainly is a very good translation). According to the Swedish text, Hammarskjöld says that faith is misunderstood if it is not seen as "a unity of self-effacement" (p. 97*). Shortly thereafter he corrects this statement by describing "a unity of self-sacrifice without self-effacement" (p. 100*).

In spite of this ambiguity the meaning of *self-surrender,* and its more or less equivalent expressions, is quite clear: in various ways they all explicate the contrast to self-centeredness. Hammarskjöld's theme is none other than the central biblical concern for losing one's life—and thereby finding it.

Yes to God is surrender to God, but precisely for that reason it includes a "yes to yourself," a formula that appears several times in *Markings*. At many points Hammarskjöld emphasizes the intimate connection between losing and finding. At one point, after having spoken about "the chaos you become whenever God's hand does not rest upon your head," he continues: "But when his attention is directed beyond and above, how strong he is, with the strength of God who is within him because he is in God. Strong and free, because his self no longer exists" (p. 96). At another point he speaks of being at once humble and proud—in faith: "Except in faith, nobody is humble. The mask of weakness or of Phariseeism is not the naked face of humility. And, except in faith, nobody is proud. The vanity displayed in all its varieties by the spiritually immature is not pride. To be, in faith, both humble and proud: that is, to *live,* to know that in God I am nothing, but that God is in me" (p. 88).

More than any others, two words explain the meaning of this yes to the self: *freedom* and *integrity*. *Markings* often demonstrates the vigorous feeling of liberation which proceeds from the yes to God: "To be free, to be able to stand up and leave *everything* behind—without looking back. To say *Yes—*" (p. 88). This freedom is a freedom from the self, from self-concern (p. 108), from fear (pp. 110, 113), a freedom vis-à-vis men: "He who has placed himself in God's hand stands free vis-à-vis men: he is entirely at his ease with them, because he has granted them the right to judge" (p. 88). The same theme returns in 1959. He begins by saying that "humility is just as much the opposite of self-abasement as it is of self-exaltation" and ends with these words: "Praise and blame, the winds of success and adversity, blow over such a life without leaving a trace or upsetting its balance. Towards this, so help me, God—" (p. 148). Freedom can also be described as liberation from things; however, to this notion Hammarskjöld adds: "but you encounter in them an experience which has the purity and clarity of revelation" (p. 139).

A prominent and striking element in Hammarskjöld's concentration on liberation is the oft-repeated theme, Do not look back. In one of the many passages where these words appear Hammarskjöld says: "to obey the order when it is given and never look back—then He can use you—then, *perhaps,* He will use you" (p. 112). Later he reminds us that "the myths have always condemned those who 'looked back'" (p. 132). Statements of this kind clearly reveal how severely Hammarskjöld had been tormented during the years of crisis. Some statements from the second period recall to mind the self-torture of that time: "Do you still need to evoke memories of a self-imposed humiliation in order to extinguish a smoldering self-admiration?" (p. 99). "Not to brood over my pettiness with masochistic self-disgust, nor to take a pride in admitting it—but to recognize it as a threat to my integrity of action, the moment I let it out of my sight" (p. 129).

Freedom and integrity are united in a passage where they stand in bright contrast to life lived in fetters: "Clad in this 'self,' the creation of irresponsible and ignorant persons, meaningless honors and catalogued acts—strapped into the strait jacket of the immediate. To step out of all this, and stand naked on the precipice of dawn—accepted, invulnerable, free: in the Light, with the Light, of the Light. *Whole,* real in the Whole [literally: *One* in the oneness]. Out of myself as a stumbling block, into myself as fulfillment" (p.130*). To be *one* or *whole* involves integrity; in fact, Hammarskjöld at times uses both words together. In writing about freedom and integrity he says: "—one with your task, whole in your duty of the moment" (p.135). The condition of being one, of integrity, is to be in God's hand; conversely, life without being in God's hand is chaos.

The integrity of the "I" is a wonder. We hear him say, "The wonder: that *I* exist" (p.102). Here, obviously, he is speaking of the integrity of this "I," the integrity of being one in union with God. But he also can invert such a statement: in God's hand every moment has its meaning; indeed, "from this perspective, to 'believe in God' is to believe in yourself, as self-evident, as 'illogical,' and as impossible to explain: if I can be, then God *is"* (p.112). Hammarskjöld uses yet another word, parallel in meaning to *one* and *whole.* Hammarskjöld says: "To be single-hearted is to experience reality, not *in relation to ourselves,* but in its sacred independence. It is to see, judge, and act from the point of rest in ourselves. Then, how much disappears, and all that remains falls into place" (p. 148*). The Swedish for *single-hearted* could be translated "simplicity" or, better, "simple-hearted." The English translation, "to have humility," does not correspond to the Swedish word. The expression "rest in ourselves" or, as he also says, "rest in the center of our being" does not, of course, mean self-centeredness—it means the exact opposite of that.

Looking back at Hammarskjöld on freedom and integrity, it is clear that these things are to be considered a gift that he has received and yet something permanently to fight for. This second outlook is underlined everywhere in *Markings:* "So long as you abide in the Unheard-of, you are beyond and above—to hold fast to this must be the First Commandment in your spiritual discipline" (p. 94); "Before God . . . you are always in the bottom class of nursery school" (p. 95); "The life of simplicity is simple, but it opens to us a book in which we never get beyond the first syllable" (p.148).

The Image of God

In his writings on the nature of faith, Hammarskjöld succeeds in speaking clearly about the meaning of union with God and life in the hands of God. Further, the attentive reader cannot help but be aware of Hammarskjöld's certainties about the proper nature of prayer. But—what is his actual image of the God in whom he believes and to whom he prays? This question seems to be more complicated. We have, to be sure, already caught a glimpse of Hammarskjöld's image of God in our examination of God's activity in relation to man's faith. However, it will now be necessary to investigate more closely what *Markings* discloses concerning the image of God.

It is most convenient first to look at the names for God used by Hammarskjöld. We can distinguish between two categories: anonymous names and titles of a precise character. To the first category belong terms such as "Someone" or even "Something"—Hammarskjöld's yes to God is a yes to Someone or Something. Other anonymous names are "the Other," "the Oneness," "the Unity." This tendency to identify God anonymously appears most strikingly in a quotation from Eckhart which asserts that we ought to love God "as if He were a non-God, a non-Spirit, a non-Person, a non-Substance: love Him simply as the One, the pure and absolute Unity in which is no trace of Duality" (p. 99). According to this declaration God ought to be described only in negative statements. The anonymous appelations used by the author of *Markings* are drawn from the writings of the medieval mystics.

In contrast, the names of the second category have their origin in the Bible. Here we ought first to observe that God is addressed as "Thou," a form of address especially used in prayers to and meditations before God. Subsequently, the chief word used to describe the character of God is *love*. Further, and quite naturally, we meet a long series of biblical expressions, many of which are to be found in the quotations from the Psalter. God is the Lord, the Father, the Creator, the creative will; in him is power and glory, he makes wonders, he "sees all"; in him is mercy and, therefore, he shall be feared.

Two definitions of faith—two types of names for God. Our discussion of the two definitions of faith revealed that, in fact, they say the same thing in different forms. It is only necessary to add that the phrase "in God's hand" accentuates "God over us" and thus prevents the phrase "union with God" from being misinterpreted to mean union between two equal parts. If, however, we compare the two definitions of faith with the two types of names for God, it must be said that these two categories of names imply·different perspectives and, therefore, their natures and the relations between them ought now to be considered.

Throughout the years the two categories appear side by side. The anonymous names do not gradually disappear. On the contrary, in his final retrospective statement from 1961 Hammarskjöld emphasizes them most strongly; here he speaks of saying yes to Someone or Something, and this attitude is repeated in a subsequent prayer which ends with these words:

> Thou
> Whom I do not know
> But Whose I am.
>
> Thou
> Whom I do not comprehend
> But who hast dedicated me
> To my destiny.
> Thou— (p. 176.)

Hammarskjöld stresses the incomprehensibility and unfathomableness of God in a way not unfamiliar to the Bible: "How unsearchable are his judgments and how inscrutable his ways!" (Rom. 11:33). Eckhart's words, too, ought to be interpreted in this perspective. We may well wonder about Hammarskjöld's reasons for citing this very typical expression of the *via negativa* of medieval mysticism. His reason was certainly not that he found these negative definitions "adequate," nor that he believed that nothing more could be said about God. He himself offered many affirmations concerning God. Rather, he quoted Eckhart because— as we have seen—he had discovered all designations of God to be ultimately inadequate and, furthermore, because he was most eager to maintain that the last word about God is *mystery*. For Hammarskjöld the importance of these strange words of the *via negativa* was precisely that they emphasized the mystery of God. Thus it is that his interpretation of Eckhart's words has direct reference to all that humans can utter about God. A word such as *non-Person* guards against anthropomorphisms which degrade God by forming and interpreting him according to human measurements. A word such as *non-Substance* guards against metaphysical or quasi-metaphysical descriptions of God as a "substance" existing somewhere in heaven.

Nevertheless, in the same quotation from Eckhart, Hammarskjöld also found another word of considerable importance to him: God is the One, "the Unity in which is no trace of Duality." The One, Oneness, the Unity are expressions which occur frequently in *Markings*—we need only recall how Hammarskjöld described the proper relation to God as "one in the Oneness." To be one in God is a notion of considerable significance: he who is in the hands of God is single-hearted, and not divided or, as in the Epistle of James, "double-minded." The opposite of being *one* is, according to Hammarskjöld, the chaos which results whenever God's hand is withdrawn. We should clearly have no difficulty understanding the meaning of "being one"; the unanswered question is, what does Hammarskjöld mean by God as the One or the pure Unity?

We discover the answer in the assertion that to be one in God as the One, the Unity, is at the same time to be in harmony with existence as a whole and to see the whole of existence as meaningful. We have observed in connection with Hammarskjöld's attitude towards nature that he felt the desire, indeed the necessity, "to find a way to chime in as one note of the organic whole."[2] It can be affirmed that this aspiration was fulfilled in the experience of God as the One, the Unity, the Whole. When Hammarskjöld asks if life has a meaning, his answer is significant: "Experience Life as reality and the question becomes meaningless. . . . Thus subordinated, your life will receive from Life all its meaning" (p. 114). Life—with a capital *L*—is here identical with existence as a whole, and to be "one in the Oneness" is to experience unity with existence and to find it meaningful.

This positive valuation of Life, however, does not mean that Hammarskjöld considered existence as thoroughly good or free from problems. On the contrary, he knows full well that evil and destructive powers are

---

[2] See pp. 26–27 above.

at work in existence, in human life. It must be observed that his view of harmony with existence as a whole is intimately connected with his view of creation, one of the chief words in *Markings*. When talking about God as creator he lays decisive weight upon the fact that God is *continually* creating—and *thus* it is that the relation to existence, to Life, can be a state of harmony, consonance, and solidarity.

The frequent use in *Markings* of anonymous titles for God does not mean that, for Hammarskjöld, God disappears in inaccessible distance. On the contrary, it is a very interesting and illuminating fact that his use of anonymous titles is often directly connected with words which express positively and definitively the nearness of God. Thus: "Thou whom I do not know but Whose I am." And again: "Only when you descend into yourself and encounter the Other, do you then experience goodness as the ultimate reality—united and living—*in* Him and *through* you" (p.139).

In considering the positive and comprehensive statements about God found in *Markings*, it is essential to limit our inquiry to two main topics: the use of *Thou* as the most frequent designation of God in Hammarskjöld's prayers and meditations; and the fact that all of Hammarskjöld's writings on the character of God can be summarized in the word *love*.

Obviously, *Thou* is the name most readily at hand when Hammarskjöld addresses God in prayer or meditation. It is the most appropriate title for a faith which can be characterized as union with God or being in God's hand. Two prayers typify Hammarskjöld's manner:

> Thou who art over us,
>
> . . . .
>
> Keep me in Thy love
> As Thou wouldest that all should be kept in mine.
> May everything in this my being be directed to Thy glory
> And may I never despair.
> For I am under Thy hand,
> And in Thee is all power and goodness.
>
> Give me a pure heart—that I may see Thee,
> A humble heart—that I may hear Thee,
> A heart of love—that I may serve Thee,
> A heart of faith—that I may abide in Thee. (p. 93)

And from his last year:

> Have mercy
> Upon us.
> Have mercy
> Upon our efforts,
> That we
> Before Thee,
> In love and in faith,
> Righteousness and humility,
> May follow Thee,
> With self-denial, steadfastness, and courage,
> And meet Thee
> In the silence. (p. 176.)

Thereupon he repeats the prayer from page 100, cited above, "Give me a pure heart," changing only the pronouns from the first person, *me* and *I*, to the second person, *us* and *we*. He concludes with his familiar formula: "Thou Whom I do not know but Whose I am."

The roots for Hammarskjöld's frequent use of *Thou* are surely to be found in the Bible. His intimate familiarity with the Psalter is revealed in his frequent quotation of that book, using always the text found in the Book of Common Prayer of the Anglican Communion. It is also worth mentioning that several times he cites the first three petitions of the Our Father, with their triple *Thy:* Thy name, Thy kingdom, Thy will. Hammarskjöld's relationship to God certainly can be described as an "I-Thou" relation. As is well known, Hammarskjöld in the last summer of his life was working on a Swedish translation of Martin Buber's *I and Thou*. It is not surprising that he had great interest in Buber and his writings and that, on his journeys to the Middle East, he took the occasion to visit the great philosopher in Jerusalem. In his essay, "Motivations and Methods of Dag Hammarskjöld,"[3] Andrew W. Cordier tells how he and Hammarskjöld together read and discussed *I and Thou*. Buber's thinking is, Cordier observes, reflected in Hammarskjöld's statement of

---

[3] Andrew W. Cordier, "Motivations and Methods of Dag Hammarskjöld," in *Paths to World Order,* ed. Andrew W. Cordier and Kenneth Maxwell (New York: Columbia University Press, 1967), p. 3.

November 1955, "You can only hope to find a lasting solution to a conflict if you have learned to see the other objectively, but, at the same time, to experience his difficulties subjectively" (p.102).

It might be appropriate here, by way of excursus, to comment on Hammarskjöld's relation to Buber. Cordier is no doubt correct in stating that Hammarskjöld had an affinity for Buber. This is confirmed by a speech of Hammarskjöld's, "The Walls of Distrust,"[4] delivered at Cambridge University in 1958. Here he quotes at length from Buber, actually explicating the short passage from 1955 which we have just quoted. Obviously, that brief passage reflects Buber's *I and Thou*, the book which contains his well-known distinction between the two different kinds of relationship: I-Thou and I-It. The words "to see the other objectively" refer to the I-it relation, and the words "to experience the difficulties subjectively" refer to the I-Thou relation. To take the I-Thou relation with sufficient seriousness is—Hammarskjöld says—an aid in overcoming the "walls of distrust."

However, it is very difficult to point out in *Markings* a more direct influence from Buber. In his discussion of this theme Van Dusen points out a change which took place in Buber's thinking: in his earlier years mysticism meant much to him, but he later felt that the position of mysticism was too negative at the point of life in the world. "I lack," says Buber, "the mystic's negation . . . . I am enormously concerned with just this world, this painful and precious fullness of all that I see, hear, taste."[5]

However, according to Van Dusen, Hammarskjöld was already, "before his personal meeting with Buber, suspicious of conventional mystic claims."[6] For an indication of this suspicion, Van Dusen refers to Hammarskjöld's statement about "a contact with reality, light and intense like the touch of a loved hand: a union in self-surrender without self-destruction . . . . How different from what the knowing ones call Mysticism" (p. 100). Van Dusen holds that Hammarskjöld is here speaking of himself; others assert that he is talking about Jesus. In this connection, how-

---

[4] Dag Hammarskjöld, "The Walls of Distrust," in *Servant of Peace*, ed. Wilder Foote (New York: Harper, 1962), pp. 184–87.
[5] Martin Buber, quoted in Van Dusen, *Dag Hammarskjöld*, pp. 186–87.
[6] Van Dusen, *Dag Hammarskjöld*, p. 188.

ever, it is not necessary to discuss that question; I shall return later to this most difficult and variously interpreted passage. Suffice it to say that Van Dusen is right in saying that the passage shows Hammarskjöld's openness towards the world, towards reality.[7] The statement was written about two months prior to the November 1955 passage which we identified in terms of its affinity to Buber. While it thus might also have been influenced by Buber, there is no compelling evidence for that assumption. In fact, Van Dusen is even more correct than he thinks. The last words in the passage, "the knowing ones," ought to be interpreted as ironical. The "knowing ones" are they who have interpreted the mystics traditionally, emphasizing their negative attitude to the world. Hammarskjöld himself *never* interpreted them in this way. Whether or not he was correct in his judgment is not crucial; the relevant question is *how* he interpreted them and *what* he discovered in their writings which was personally important.

The answer is quite clear, as we can see in his retrospective statement of 1953. He stresses the mystics' "strength to say *yes* to every demand which the needs of their neighbors made them face, and to say *yes* also to every fate life had in store for them when they followed the call of duty, as they understood it." The love that filled them to self-oblivion "found natural expressions in an unhesitant fulfillment of duty and in an unreserved acceptance of life."[8] Thus did the mystics contribute to Hammarskjöld. And this corresponded to the attitude of duty and service that was his own long before he met Martin Buber and, also, long before he read Albert Schweitzer.

It is not surprising that Hammarskjöld became interested in Buber. He obviously was drawn to Buber's thinking, and he appreciated Buber's ability clearly to present thoughts he himself had tried to formulate: "Martin Buber has found expressions which it would be vain for me to try to improve."[9] But it could hardly be said that Hammarskjöld's views were changed by Buber. When he encountered Buber, his way of thinking was already fully developed. Nevertheless, the main idea in Buber's *I and Thou* was of considerable import for him.

---

[7] Ibid., pp. 185–89.
[8] Dag Hammarskjöld, "Old Creeds in a New World," in *Servant of Peace* (see n. 4 above), p. 24.
[9] Hammarskjöld, "Walls of Distrust," p. 187.

Let us then return to our main topic, the image of God and Hammarskjöld's use of the pronoun *Thou* in addressing God. Buber's distinction between the relationships illuminates not only "the walls of distrust" but also—and not least—man's proper relation to God. Buber, of course, was not the one who taught Hammarskjöld to address God as Thou; that he had learned from the Bible. From Buber's philosophy Hammarskjöld got what might be called a framework for his own thoughts. This meant a stronger accent on the fact that the proper relation to God was a relation of the I to a transsubjective Thou. In the light of this primary relation all statements *about* God must be considered secondary; they refer, perhaps, to an I-it relation—an insight that corresponds to Hammarskjöld's view that there are no adequate determinations for God.

Love is a "much misused and misinterpreted word," Hammarskjöld wrote in 1953. This word is undoubtedly primary for all that he has to say about the character of God, albeit he used other woods—*goodness, mercy, grace, light*—as parallels to *love* or as expressions of elements in the love of God: only when you "encounter the Other, do you then experience goodness as the ultimate reality" (p.139), as God.

In any discussion of the role of love in Hammarskjöld's view of God, the prayers in *Markings* are most important. The most important thing is "to love life and men as God loves them—for the sake of their infinite possibilities" (p. 112).

Again,

> Every hour
> Eye to eye
> With this love
> Which sees all
> But overlooks
> In patience,
> Which is justice,
> But does not condemn
> If our glances
> Mirror its own
> In humility. (p. 121.)

It must be remembered that to Hammarskjöld humility in the context of love always meant virtually the same thing as self-surrender.

It hardly needs to be pointed out that the love of God is something quite different from laxity or flaccidity. To interpret love in such a way would be horribly to misunderstand the authentic meaning of God's love. On the contrary: "The religious reality [God] . . . forces the 'Night Side' out into the light." To stand before God is to "stand in the righteous all-seeing light of love . . . . A living relation to God is the necessary precondition for the self-knowledge which enables us to follow a straight path" (p. 128). This view of the proper relation to God appears with great frequency in *Markings*. To be sure, Hammarskjöld does not often speak of God as Father—that happens only in certain trinitarian statements—but it is interesting to note that when it appears that title is almost always connected with the thought of God's righteousness. God is a scrutinizing Father: *"Before* Thee, Father, / In righteousness and humility" (p. 109). We remember that once he spoke about a Confucian kind of trinity: "looking straight into one's own heart— / (as we can do in the mirror-image of the Father)" (p. 117).

On the other hand, God's love is essentially creating and giving. This side of God's love appears whenever Hammarskjöld writes of the relation to God as God's union with the soul or in terms of the hands of God. Such a relation to God is a gift of love—yet this gift and the claims of God are indissolubly united. The way in which, in the final prayer of *Markings,* Hammarskjöld expresses the activity of God's "grace" and his "strictness" is most significant: "By Thy mercy / Abase me, / By Thy strictness / Raise me up" (p. 178).

"Light" is one of the symbols in *Markings* which refer to the divine. "Wind" is another, mainly used in reference to the Spirit of God. In 1956 we meet both symbols, joined together. Hammarskjöld first quotes the Gospel of John (3:8, 1:5). "The *Wind* bloweth where it listeth— / so is everyone that is born of the spirit"; "And the *light* shineth in darkness, / and the darkness comprehended it not." Then he explains the two words: "Like wind— In it, with it, *of* it. Of it just like a sail, so light and strong that, even when it is bent flat, it gathers all the power of the wind without hampering its course." The Johannine text about the light, a reference to Christ as the "Word" of God, is interpreted as the light of God transforming man: "Like light— In light, lit through by light, transformed into light. Like the lens which disappears in the light it focuses" (p. 112). He who is of the wind and "lit through by light" is borne away by the wind and disappears in the light.

The figure of the lens returns in another passage about the light: "You are not the oil, you are not the air—merely the point of combustion, the flash-point where the light is born. You are merely the lens in the beam. You can only receive, give, and possess the light as a lens does. If you seek yourself . . . you rob the lens of its transparency" (p. 133). Obviously, light is a symbol of the love of God. The light is a transforming and liberating power—at another point Hammarskjöld speaks about being free in the light. It is hardly possible to read Hammarskjöld in these passages without remembering two biblical texts about "the light": "Let your light so shine before men, that they may see your good works and give glory to your Father who is in heaven" (Matt. 5:16); and "God is light and in him is no darkness at all" (1 John 1:5). Hammarskjöld did not quote these texts—why should he?—but, in fact, he explains them. The text about God as light without any darkness could well stand as a correct explanation of that passage from Eckhart which is so crucial to *Markings:* God is "pure and absolute Unity in which is no trace of Duality."

God and Christ

"A Brother to follow"—during the years of his spiritual crisis Hammarskjöld's contemplations brought him to that affirmation concerning Jesus. And in 1961 he writes that "step by step" he had learned more and more about the "hero of the Gospels." Now, what had he actually learned?

A development in Hammarskjöld's view of Jesus is surely to be found in the progression of *Markings*. Furthermore, since this was a genuine development we must caution against considering the view of Jesus found in the second part of *Markings* to be a view which stands in contrast to Hammarskjöld's original position from which he was once persuaded to follow the Crucified on the way of self-sacrifice. It is, accordingly, appropriate that we first consider his original picture of Jesus as the basis for examining his ultimate encounter with "the hero of the

Gospels." Most striking in this original picture is the certainty that the Jesus whom he decided to follow was a human being among human beings, "a young man, adamant in his commitment to life." The self-sacrifice of this Jesus was complete, thoroughly a sacrifice "for the sake of others." His decision was risky, and he stood quite alone, "even sacrificing affection and fellowship when the others are unready to follow him." This view of Jesus does return in *Markings* from time to time: Jesus is always a young man, adamant in his commitment to life, always the man who sacrifices himself and, as such, the Brother worth following. In point of fact, the view of Jesus presented in the second part of *Markings* is consistently determined—albeit in various ways—by his sacrifice.

Sacrifice is the key word. Before we look at Hammarskjöld's picture of Jesus, it is suitable to consider the meaning of sacrifice to Hammarskjöld himself. To be in God's hands, in union with God, means from the side of man a self-surrender which is indissolubly connected with self-sacrifice. The example of Jesus has shown that it must be a self-sacrifice without reservation and for the sake of others. In the light of union with God, Hammarskjöld sees "that the 'offering' is here and now, always and everywhere—'surrendered' *to be* what, in me, God gives of Himself to Himself" (p. 91). "In the last analysis, what does the word 'sacrifice' mean? Or even the word 'gift'? He who has nothing can give nothing. The gift is God's—to God" (p. 88). This latter statement was made in 1953, the year of his *yes*. But the same outlook is stressed even more strongly on his birthday in 1958: "Still a few years more, and then? The only value of a life is its content for *others*. Apart from any value it may have for others, my life is worse than death. Therefore—in my great loneliness—serve others. Therefore: how incredibly great is what I have been given, and what nothingness that which I have to 'sacrifice' " (p. 140*). Nevertheless, even if in this perspective it is "nothingness," the reality of sacrifice has decisive weight for *all* the questions of life: "In the last analysis, it is our conception of sacrifice [not "death," as in the English translation] which decides our answers to all the questions that life puts to us. That is why it requires its proper place and time—if need be, with right of precedence" (p. 136*).

The sacrifice is a sacrifice "for the sake of others," and it must be realized in service to others, in self-surrender and in self-oblivion. In writing about self-oblivion Hammarskjöld says: "'Thine . . .' A sacrifice—and a liberation—to obey a will for which 'I' is in no respect a goal!" (p. 98). This is the *"imitatio"* of Jesus. In a meditation on Jesus Hammarskjöld describes the signification of His example:

> With the love of Him who knows all,
> With the patience of Him Whose now is eternal,
> With the righteousness of Him who has never failed,
> With the humility of Him who has suffered all the possibilities
>   of betrayal. (p. 118)

This demand of service in complete self-oblivion provoked in Hammarskjöld a perpetual self-critique. The self-critique that was so apparent in the years of crisis did not diminish when he had said his *yes* to God; on the contrary, it increased, as almost every page of *Markings* indicates. Hammarskjöld fought self-centeredness in all its shapes, pursuing it to the deepest and most secret corners: "So, once again, you chose for yourself—and opened the door to chaos" (p. 95). His enemies included the propensity "furtively to seek honor for yourself," and "a tone of voice which places you in the limelight." "If you go on in this way, thoughtlessly mirroring yourself in an obituary, you will soon be writing your epitaph —in two senses" (p.109). "If only the goal can justify the sacrifice, how, then, can you attach a shadow of importance to the question whether or not the memory of your efforts will be associated with your name? If you do, is it not all too obvious that you are still being influenced in your actions by that vain dead dream about 'posterity'?" (p. 122). He accuses himself of solipsism, greed for power, pettiness, the desire to keep himself well to the fore; of being joyless and, thus, a killer of joy. At one point, when writing about his work, he admonishes himself against two dangers: "Living submerged in this heavy *Fluidum* of the sub-human— sub-human in insight, feeling, and energy—beware of twofold danger— of drowning and of floating—of lowering yourself until this position below the clear surface of the truly human seems to you the natural one, and of upholding your banner in a vacuum of 'superiority' " (p.120).

A self-critique that returns several times concerns the "destruction-instinct" (in the English this is translated as "death-instinct" or "death-wish." The theme of death certainly appears often in *Markings*, but the word *destruction* most characteristically represents the evil which stands in contrast to creation, the divine—God and his love): "What really matters is to be *only* under God: the slightest division of allegiance opens the door to daydreaming, petty conversation, petty boasting, petty malice —all the petty satellites of the destruction-instinct" (p. 99*). Again: "It is when we stand in the righteous all-seeing light of love that we can dare to look at, admit, and *consciously* suffer under this something in us which wills disaster, misfortune, defeat to everything outside the sphere of our narrowest self-interest" (p. 128). Not least do the prayers in *Markings* bear witness to Hammarskjöld's hard, never ceasing self-examination, and his constant battle against self-centeredness.

His critical self-examination and his earnest awareness of shortcomings emphasized for Hammarskjöld the distance between his sacrifice and Jesus', the complete self-surrender "for the sake of others." The result was that Hammarskjöld began to see Jesus from yet another point of view. Certainly he remained an example to follow, a human being among human beings, a Brother on the way forward. But at the same time his way of self-sacrifice did reveal the quality of love that is really divine—and this love was the power of God acting in his sacrifice. This position, as unfolded in *Markings*, is by no means a contradiction of Hammarskjöld's general view of the significance of sacrifice; on the contrary, this position is quite in line with that general view. Sacrifice is always a sacrifice for the sake of others, bearing the burdens of others; thus sacrifice always has a vicarious character.

Let us now consider the view of Jesus presented in the second part of *Markings*. We must first return to a passage already examined in our consideration of mysticism and reality. Curiously, the original Swedish text includes at this point two entries—which in the English translation have been combined into one. This combination has, perhaps, not been without influence upon Van Dusen's view that the entire passage is about Hammarskjöld himself.[10] It will be necessary to quote the passage in its entirety according to its Swedish form.

[10] Van Dusen, *Dag Hammarskjöld*, p. 133.

He broke fresh ground [literally: a new way]—because, and only because, he had the courage to go ahead without asking whether others were following or even understood. He had no need for the divided responsibility in which others seek to be safe from ridicule, because he had been granted a faith which required no confirmation.

—a contact with reality, light and intense like the touch of a loved hand: a union in self-surrender without self-destruction, where his heart was lucid and his mind loving. In sun and wind, how near and how remote— How different from what the knowing ones call Mysticism. (p. 100*.)

The first part, at least, of this double entry must have Jesus for its subject. Familiar elements are present which are integral to Hammarskjöld's picture of Jesus: solitude, no care whether others followed or understood, the faith which required no confirmation. It also ought to be observed that Hammarskjöld's usual practice is to refer to himself as "you," not as "he." Thus, Jesus is presented as a model for action, one able to break fresh ground and, therefore, one whose way of action is a way to be followed. In the second entry the author meditates over the significance of this way of action: it means a contact with reality through a self-surrender which is not self-destruction. That, indeed, is exactly what Hammarskjöld finds in "Mysticism"—not the flight from reality that "the knowing ones" customarily consider to be a hallmark of mysticism.

The next statement concerning Jesus which we must consider has also already appeared in our study; we quoted it when examining Hammarskjöld's view of the non-Christian religions.[11] This passage, written on Good Friday 1956, is one of the many sections of *Markings* written on the great festival days of the Church Year. The events of Good Friday are followed hour by hour. And simultaneously the past is changed into the present, into an eternal *now,* and Jesus "dies" in someone—in everyone—"who has followed the trail marks of the inner road to the end." An immense weight is here laid upon the event at Golgotha; yet the predominant role remains *imitatio*—to watch and to follow on the way of sacrifice.

---

[11] See pp. 48–49 above.

In yet another section of *Markings* we meet the same demand; this time, however, a new dimension concerning the "offering," which in Swedish is the same word as "sacrifice." The two verses run:

> May I be offered
> To that in the offering
> Which will be offered.
>
> God took the form of man
> In the victim
> Who chose to be sacrificed. (p. 158.)

"God took the form of man"—the old-fashioned Swedish words here used by Hammarskjöld are the same as those found in the Swedish text of the Nicene Creed. The decision to be sacrificed reveals the meaning—we could say, the deepest meaning—of the divine love, and Hammarskjöld designates this revelation as the authentic key to the "incarnation" of God. Considerable discussion has arisen about this statement, and some have even characterized it as "heretical." Now, such a characterization would have had no interest at all for Hammarskjöld himself, and nothing will be served by adopting such terms for our discussion. Still, the passage itself helps us better to understand Hammarskjöld's intentions. It must be pointed out first that here we find the same stress upon the free decision of Jesus that appears so consistently in *Markings*. Certainly, without that decision and the ensuing sacrifice Hammarskjöld would never have written of an "incarnation." Nevertheless, he clearly has no intention of isolating this decision from Jesus' life-achievement as a whole; the decision and sacrifice is the fulfillment of Jesus' life-work and thus also the fulfillment of the "incarnation." This point of view, indeed, is not peculiar to Hammarskjöld; it can be found often in the history of theology and is frequently discovered in the theology of our own time, although Hammarskjöld probably never was aware of it. Second, we must approach this verse in its relation to *Markings* as a whole. For instance, Hammarskjöld, in referring to the Gospel of John, speaks of Jesus as the light shining in the darkness, and on Christmas Eve of 1960 he writes: "How proper it is that Christmas should follow

Advent. —For him who looks towards the future, the Manger is situated on Golgotha, and the Cross has already been raised in Bethlehem" (p. 163). The fulfillment has its roots in the beginning, and that which was from the beginning was decisively disclosed and made apparent in the fulfillment. The whole life-achievement of Jesus is to be seen as an incarnation of the love of God—of God in man.

Hammarskjöld's thoughts on the significance of the sacrifice of Jesus are further illustrated by his use of two Swedish hymns. Sadly, the English translation of *Markings* has completely misunderstood the first of these, and the meaning of the second is by no means crystal clear. The first hymn appears as the first entry for 1955. It is a Passion hymn, "Du bar ditt kors, o Jesus mild" ("Thy cross, O Jesus, Thou didst bear") by one of the most remarkable figures of nineteenth century Swedish intellectual history: Erik Gustaf Geijer, historian, philosopher, poet, and musician. In the Swedish, Hammarskjöld's quotation begins with a dash; then follow the words, "for there is nothing that is not won" (literally translated), and after that three dashes. Translated into prose, the whole verse reads roughly: "Thou didst bear thy cross. Thy glory which is praised by all heavens, Thy power without limits, Thou laid aside — thus to show that *there is nothing that is not won* by the love which suffers." Hammarskjöld is here obviously considering the victorious power of the suffering love of Christ. The English translation has obscured totally the significant words concealed behind the dashes which are found in the Swedish text. In translation the verse reads: "Nought is given 'neath the sun, / Nought is had that is not won" (p. 95). If this translation has any meaning at all, it is certainly not that which was important for Hammarskjöld.

The second hymn, quoted at Christmas 1960, is from the most famous Swedish Christmas hymn, written by the great hymnist and poet, Archbishop J. O. Wallin. The English translation runs:

> Strive, the pains of death endure,
> Peace eternal to secure:
> For the faithful and the tried
> Heaven's Gates shall open wide. (p. 163.)

In this version, the verse might be interpreted as one which deals with human striving and faithfulness. However, that is grossly incorrect. It will be necessary again to translate the Swedish verse into literal English prose: "His [Christ's] eyes, as ours, will be filled with tears. He will understand our need and help us by the power of his Spirit, announce to us the council of his Father, and mix the sweetness of eternal grace in the chalice of sorrow—strive, endure the pains of death so that our heart may win peace and find an opened heaven." These two quotations speak for themselves. Both are important for Hammarskjöld's interpretation of the significance of the sacrifice: it was a sacrifice "for the sake of others" and thus a vicarious sacrifice which brought help to others, "breaking a new way"; it was, indeed, the love of God in action.

Two additional entries from 1960 concerning Jesus are worth our attention: a verse written in November of that year (p. 165) and the entry for Easter (p. 163). The poetry does not require special comment. It is sufficient to say that it shows how intimately Hammarskjöld was committed to the way of Jesus towards the cross and that it also shows how intensely Hammarskjöld was occupied with the thoughts that his own way was to be one of sacrifice.

On the other hand, the Easter passage is undoubtedly one of *Markings'* more discussed sections—perhaps the most discussed. "Forgiveness breaks the chain of causality because he who 'forgives' you—out of love—takes upon himself the responsibility for the consequences of what *you* have done. Forgiveness, therefore, always entails a sacrifice. The price you must pay for your own liberation through another's sacrifice is that you in turn must be willing to liberate in the same way, irrespective of the consequences to yourself" (p. 163*).

The issue here is obviously the relation between forgiveness and sacrifice. Before we attempt an interpretation, therefore, it will be necessary to investigate what Hammarskjöld has previously said about forgiveness. In point of actual fact, the problem of forgiveness had occupied him intensely in the preceeding years, and it is possible to discern a remarkable change in his attitude.

We have seen that Hammarskjöld's yes to God included at the same time a yes to himself, chiefly apparent as a new freedom and integrity.

To be in God's hand and in union with him meant, no doubt, being accepted by God and, thus, having received forgiveness. Nevertheless, the issue of forgiveness seems to become more and more important in *Markings*. That in itself is not surprising; such an attitude corresponds to the ordinary Christian experience: forgiveness is not forgiveness once and forever, it must be repeated "daily," as long as life lasts. In light of Hammarskjöld's intense self-criticism, it is no wonder that he found the question of forgiveness most vexing.

In 1956 he wrote: "Forgiveness is the answer to the child's dream of a miracle by which what is broken is made whole again, what is soiled is again made clean. The dream explains why we need to be forgiven, and why we must forgive. In the presence of God, nothing stands between Him and us—we *are* forgiven. But we *cannot* feel His presence if anything is allowed to stand between ourselves and others" (p. 110). Here forgiveness is identical with being "in the presence of God," being in union with him. Further, forgiveness cannot be received if we fail to forgive others, a point emphasized often in the Gospels. In 1957 Hammarskjöld returned to the problem: "A living relation to God is the necessary precondition for the self-knowledge which enables us to follow a straight path, and so be victorious and be forgiven—over ourselves [important words which have a meaning different from that conveyed in the English translation] and by ourselves" (p. 128*). Here there is a double forgiveness: one "over ourselves," that is, given by God, and one that we give ourselves. Obviously, Hammarskjöld holds that to say yes to oneself, in some way, includes forgiving oneself. But he later asks: "How am I to find the strength to live as a free man, detached from all that was unjust in my past and all that is petty in my present, and so, daily, to forgive myself?" (p. 129). Ultimately, however, he indicates— in the same year—that he has changed his mind: "'To forgive oneself'—? No, that doesn't work: we have to *be forgiven*. But we can only believe this is possible if we ourselves forgive" (p. 133*). To say yes to oneself does not mean to become able to forgive ourselves. Forgiveness is completely a gift of God—but, certainly, a gift including the duty to forgive others.

Having considered this view of forgiveness, we now return to the statement of Easter 1960, where Hammarskjöld deals with the relation between forgiveness and sacrifice—with sacrifice a precondition of forgiveness. How is this passage to be interpreted? God's forgiveness is here, as always, a gift, but a gift in some way connected with sacrifice. We must ask whether Hammarskjöld's position, as we have explained it, ought to be considered a continuation of, or a deviation from, his earlier position. Commenting on the Easter 1960 passage, Van Dusen says that it "deals with the more inward and mysterious meaning of Jesus' death stressed in classic explanations of 'Christ's work.' "[12] In marked contrast to this cautious view is the position of the prominent Swedish commentator Hjalmar Sundén, who holds that this passage represents a deviation from Hammarskjöld's usual thought and that here he has accepted "the dogma of *satisfactio vicaria*." According to this interpreter, an earlier "undogmatic" view has been replaced by a "dogmatic" and "orthodox" position.[13]

Any interpretation of this Easter "Road Mark" ought to start with the words, "forgiveness always entails a sacrifice." This is a rule applicable not only to human but also to divine forgiveness. In the first part of the entry Hammarskjöld writes of the relation between divine forgiveness and sacrifice; in the second part, he stresses his familiar conviction about the necessary connection between divine forgiveness and our forgiveness of others—the price for liberation "through another's sacrifice," that is, the sacrifice of Jesus, is to "be willing to liberate in the same way, irrespective of the consequences to yourself." What does Hammarskjöld mean when, in the first part of the entry, he says, "Forgiveness breaks the chain of causality because he who 'forgives' you—out of love—takes upon himself the responsibility for the consequences of what *you* have done"?

There is no point in our discussing whether Hammarskjöld is here speaking of God *or* Christ. The word *sacrifice,* of course, has primary reference to Jesus, but at the same time it refers to the love of God. Further, even if Christ is presented as "he who forgives," the forgiveness still remains God's own, since Christ is the bearer of God's forgiveness. The somewhat unclear words about breaking "the chain of causality"

---

[12] Van Dusen, *Dag Hammarskjöld,* p. 199.
[13] Hjalmar Sundén, *Kristusmeditationer i Dag Hammarskjölds Vägmärken* (Stockholm: Verbum, 1966), p. 73.

and taking "upon himself the responsibility" ought to be interpreted as referring to the human debt: to be liberated by forgiveness is to be liberated from the debt caused by self-centeredness and its actions—thus, "the chain of causality" is broken by forgiveness.

The chief thing here is that Hammarskjöld sees the sacrifice of Christ as a manifestation of love and of the love of God—everything that has happened and that now happens is an action "out of love." Surely, this point of view by no means deviates from that which is found elsewhere in *Markings*. Hammarskjöld's central idea of sacrifice is always that it is an action "for the sake of others" and, in this sense, a "vicarious action." This idea he consistently applies to Jesus—as, for example, in his use of the two Swedish hymns which we have discussed. His position is always that sacrifice contains a power to liberate—at one point, he writes about "the creative act of sacrifice" (p.140*; this formula has not been literally translated in the English text). Indeed, no expression can better illustrate Hammarskjöld's view of the power of sacrifice: he holds that God creates by means of sacrifice.

In light of these comments, Van Dusen's statement that the Easter passage reveals an affinity with the "classic explanation" of Christ's sacrifice can be confirmed—especially if we correlate Hammarskjöld's statement more with biblical assertions than with later theological explanations. But at the same time it must be emphatically argued that there is not the slightest reason for saying that Hammarskjöld accepts "the dogma of *satisfactio vicaria*." The standard meaning of that doctrine is that God through the suffering of Christ received a satisfaction, a sufficient compensation for the sin of humanity, and that God thereby was "placated" and "reconciled." A doctrine of that kind is quite irreconcilable with the image of God found in *Markings*. The idea that the God of love needed to be changed is inconceivable to Hammarskjöld. At quite another point stands the importance that sacrifice—and sacrifice as vicarious—has in *Markings*. There is a fundamental difference between *satisfactio vicaria* and what could be called *sacrificium vicarium*. The importance of sacrifice "for the sake of others" and, consequently, of the sacrifice of Christ takes on a progressively greater role in *Markings,* but that does not involve a deviation or a transition to a new and different or "orthodox" view. What, indeed, would the word *orthodox* mean in this connection? Terms of that kind are hardly helpful for an understanding of Hammarskjöld. He himself never thought in such categories.

Finally, let us summarize the role of Christ in *Markings*. Hammarskjöld's starting point is Jesus' risky choice of self-sacrifice—for the sake of others. Risk is crucial; if the choice had not been a risky one, Jesus would not have been a human being among other human beings and his "commandment" could not have had the compelling force it now possesses. Jesus' demand that we sacrifice ourselves for the sake of others is at the same time God's own demand. Thus, Jesus reveals to us what life in union with God claims. But the sacrifice of Christ our Brother is also seen from another point of view: he not only encounters us with demands, he is also the Brother who confers on us gifts from God. The way of sacrifice is the way of love, and therefore sacrifice is a victorious and creative power which reveals the mysterious depths of God—the forgiving love that unites us with God and encloses us in God's hands. Thus it is that Hammarskjöld can say that "God took the form of man / In the victim / Who chose to be sacrificed" (p. 158). And thus it is that Christ our Brother appears in trinitarian formula, Father—Brother—Spirit, and on one occasion also as "the Son."

In all of this Christ plays a decisive role in the relationship between God and man. However, in all that Hammarskjöld says, Christ is never the end point of his thought. His intention is always to turn his eyes to God. The central thing is the relation to Him who is "the first and the last." We are familiar, in recent theology, with a certain reluctance to speak of man's relation to God: Christ has more or less taken the place of God himself, and, indeed, there has even appeared—now seemingly, and happily, laid to rest—what we called the God-is-dead theology. Such attitudes were totally alien to Hammarskjöld. The role of Christ is the role that he possesses as the one who reveals the depth of God's love—which, precisely as it is revealed, remains always a mystery.

Destiny and the Meaning of Life

In 1957 Hammarskjöld wrote: "*Yes* to God: yes to destiny, yes to yourself" (p. 135*). Yes to God is the decisive affirmation—one that includes the other two. "Destiny," the object of the second yes, is referred to often in *Markings,* where its connection with God is intimate. It is important that we see both what this connection means and what it does not mean. A clue is to be found in two passages: in the phrase, "faith which makes saying Yes to destiny a self-evident necessity" (p. 99*), and in the trinitarian meditation, "*Before* Thee, Father, / In righteousness and humility, / *With* Thee, Brother, / In faith and courage, / *In* Thee, Spirit, / In stillness." Hammarskjöld concludes this meditation in the following way: "*Thine*—for Thy will is my destiny, / Dedicated—for my destiny is to be used and used up according to Thy will" (p. 109).

When Hammarskjöld speaks of destiny he does not mean fatalism. He certainly does not hold that all that happens proceeds from God or expresses the divine will. Rather, when Hammarskjöld says that God is his destiny he is making the affirmation that in everything that happens he encounters a demand from God that must be answered. This point is made clear when he addresses God in this way: "Thou who has created us free, Who seest all that happens—yet art confident of victory" (p. 92). Properly understood, this passage says that, in spite of everything that happens in the world, in spite of the fact that much of what happens is contrary and even hostile to God's will, God nevertheless remains confident that the fight will end with his victory. When God, therefore, is occasionally addressed as "Almighty," Hammarskjöld does not imply that all occurrences must be interpreted as coming from God, as representing his will or demonstrating his power; the title *Almighty* means rather that victory belongs to God and that the final outcome will demonstrate the ultimacy of his power.

This view of God and the course of the world's events is elaborated in another entry in *Markings:* "That piece of blasphemous anthropomorphism: the belief that, in order to educate us, God wishes us to suffer. How far from this is the assent to suffering when it strikes us *because* we have obeyed what we have seen to be God's will" (p. 138*). The idea that God wishes us to suffer in order to educate us, a classical rational explanation for suffering, is dismissed as blasphemy. Suffering obviously has its origin in the world and in the evil doings of men. The principal question is whether we obey the will of God even when our obedience results in suffering.

DESTINY AND THE MEANING OF LIFE

The problem of destiny cannot be separated from the problem of good and evil—opposite categories which, Hammarskjöld emphasizes, always have reference to man: "Only in man has the creative evolution reached the point where reality encounters itself in judgment and choice. Outside of man, the creation is neither good nor evil" (p. 139*). "Creative evolution"—the use of this expression, associated so intimately with the French philosopher Henri Bergson *(L'Évolution créatrice),* may possibly indicate that Hammarskjöld had read Bergson and been influenced by his work. Seen in connection with other passages concerning creation and creative power, the expression underscores Hammarskjöld's consistent view of creation as perpetual. When man appeared in the history of creation, the categories of good and evil became relevant because man alone had the possibility of judgment and choice. If these categories are decisively important, they require that existence be seen as a drama in which good and evil struggle against each other. *Markings* is replete with illustrations of this view of life. At an early stage in the book we read: "The stream of life through millions of years, the stream of human lives through countless centuries. Evil, death and dearth, sacrifice and love" (p. 83). No doubt that means—as we have seen—that existence is a fight between evil and death and dearth, on the one side, and love and sacrifice on the other.

In this fight it is necessary for man to watch and to be prepared: "Only he who at every moment is all he is capable of being can hope for a furlough from the frontier before he disappears into the darkness. The sentinels of the Enemy do not sleep" (p. 91). In this fight no time is to be wasted: "On the field where Ormuzd has challenged Ahriman to battle, he who chases away the dogs is wasting his time" (p. 113). There is, not incidentally, good reason for Hammarskjöld's use of these names from the religion of Zoroaster: in no religion is the contrast between good and evil so strongly emphasized. In this fight everything is staked: "There are actions—justified only by faith—which can lift us into another sphere, where the battle is with 'Principalities, Dominions and Powers.' Actions upon which—out of mercy—*everything* is staked" (p. 110).

The contrast between good and evil can be described in many ways. Hardly any presentation of this contrast, however, is more significant than that which uses the terms *creating* and *destroying*. *Creating* is the word of honor, referring, of course, primarily to God who is continually creating through the power of his goodness; The opposite to creation is chaos. In God's continual creation human beings are used as instruments, and therefore the decisive question asked by Hammarskjöld of himself is: "Do you create? / Or destroy? *That's* / for your ordeal-by-fire to answer" (p. 158). Here is the inescapable responsibility. "Your responsibility is indeed terrifying. If you fail, it is God, thanks to your having betrayed Him, who will fail mankind. You fancy you can be responsible *to* God: can you carry the responsibility *for* God?" (p. 133). The contrast between creation and destruction is, further, a contrast between God and devil: "In the Devil's pack, the cards of malediction and destruction lie next to the cards of success. It is only the cards of love which are missing— Does He himself understand that this is the reason why he decides the destiny of so many? For one, he is a God-surrogate. For another, a tyrant who must be fought" (p. 79*).

When we return to the word *destiny* itself, we see that the word can be used in two senses. It can mean the happenings in which we become involved, the circumstances in which we are placed—but that does not disclose the full meaning of the term. When Hammarskjöld says that "God's will is my destiny," the word obviously means something more. It does not mean only in passivity to accept that which meets us; destiny itself faces man with a "challenge" (p. 132*)—it is always connected with a choice to be made by man. This view of destiny appears as early as 1950: "We are not permitted to choose the frame of our destiny. But what we put into it is ours. He who wills adventure will experience it— according to the measure of his courage. He who wills sacrifice will be sacrificed—according to the measure of his purity of heart" (p. 63). This perspective returns throughout *Markings*. To accept destiny does not mean merely to accept our circumstances with resignation; it means to accept that which, precisely in those circumstances, God desires us to perform. Thus Hammarskjöld writes of following "destiny's cry of exhortation" (p. 107*; this distinctive expression is completely missed in the English translation, which contents itself with the pallid "to follow this call"). Destiny means a challenge, a duty to be performed without treachery: in "the role assigned us by destiny, how strait must be our path at all times if we are not to perish" (p. 127*). Again: "A troubled spirit? Isn't the cause obvious? As soon as, furtively, you sought honor for yourself, you . . . lost that certainty of faith which makes saying Yes to destiny a self-evident necessity, for such certainty presupposes that it is not grounded in any sort of treachery" (p. 99*).

In summary: It is never to be forgotten that the yes to destiny is included in the yes to God. This does not require, as already pointed out, that we are to see every occurrence as a reflection of the will of God; there are also destructive powers at work in the drama of existence. It means, rather, that in every event of life there is a meaning supplied by God, to be realized by man. In that sense, to say yes to destiny is to say yes to God and to his will—and thus life becomes meaningful and destiny is not a chilly and meaningless fate. Life takes on meaning when destiny is seen as reflecting the will of God and operative in the choice of man.

Destiny and *fate*—the English language has two words at its disposal; the Swedish language, only one. In *Markings* both of the English expressions have been used, although in most cases the translators have chosen the word *fate*. When I have quoted Hammarskjöld, I have usually preferred to use the word *destiny* because the active implication of *destiny* and *destination* seems far more congruent with Hammarskjöld's emphasis on the will of God and the choice of man than does the dismal notion of fate and fatalism.

In a previous chapter we discussed the questions which tormented Hammarskjöld during the years of his spiritual crisis. We found that his thoughts were chiefly engaged by the problems of self-centeredness, loneliness, and meaninglessness. Now we can ask, What did Hammarskjöld's yes mean in reference to these problems? We have seen that his fight against self-centeredness never ceased. Certainly, however, a change can be observed in that the tendencies to self-contempt disappeared. But self-criticism did not decrease. On the contrary, self-criticism was ruthlessly accentuated, and Hammarskjöld knew why. It was accentuated before the eye of righteous love; the experience of "religious reality" forced the "Night Side" into the light. Nor did the loneliness disappear.

There are many passages in *Markings* which speak of this loneliness— passages which have led many to gross misunderstanding. In point of fact, it is easy to substantiate the assertion that Hammarskjöld had no difficulty in cooperating with others and that he did not lack friends. The loneliness that he confesses in *Markings* has a deeper root and a deeper significance. It is, even in his later years, a loneliness that cannot be cured through cooperation or friendship. To this loneliness his answer is double-sided: in God, he says first, is he never alone; and in service, he says second, is to be found a place of abode. "Forever among strangers to all that has shaped your life—*alone*. Forever thirsting for the living waters—but not even free to seek them, a *prisoner*. The answer—the hard straight severe answer: in the One you are never alone, in the One you are always at home" (p. 132*). A hard answer—and he asks, "Did'st Thou give me this inescapable loneliness so that it would be easier for me to give Thee all?" (p. 139). Thereupon, he immediately concludes: "Therefore, in my great loneliness, serve others. Therefore: how incredibly great is what I have been given, and how meaningless what I have to 'sacrifice' " (p. 140).

Concerning the question of the meaning of life, however, Hammarskjöld's answer is clear, positive, and unhesitating. In the crucial statement of Whitsunday 1961 he states that, when once he had said yes to "Someone—or Something," from that hour "I was certain that existence is meaningful and that, therefore, my life, in self-surrender, had a goal" (p. 169).

That life is meaningful is often asserted in *Markings:* "You dare your Yes—and experience a meaning. You repeat your Yes—and all things acquire a meaning. When everything has a meaning, how can you live anything but a *Yes*" (p. 110). The meaning of life stands firm, and independent of all eventualities. When Hammarskjöld has written that, if you do obey the order, God *perhaps* will use you, he continues: "And if he doesn't use you—what matter. In His hand, every moment has its meaning, its greatness, its glory, its peace, its co-inherence" (p. 112). That the meaning of life is independent of its conditions is also underscored: "You will find that, thus subordinated, your life will receive from Life all its meaning, irrespective of the conditions given you for its realization" (p. 114). Quoting from French, Hammarskjöld speaks of destiny as being at once a mystery and a source of meaning for life: "Destiny is something not to be desired and not to be avoided . . . it is a mystery not contrary to reason, for it implies that the world, and the course of human history, have meaning" (p. 124).

It is, finally and in light of this whole picture of destiny and life's meaning, no wonder that in *Markings* we find neither accusations against God nor tendencies to defend him. No theodicy, no speculations about the origin of evil. To attempt a defense of God would be as meaningless as to accuse him. Here Hammarskjöld is consistent with his view that the decisive contrast is that between creating and destroying. The question of evil is to be answered by combatting it. The anchor of hope and the ground of life's meaning is given in faith in the God who, in spite of all that happens, is confident of victory.

Chapter Five

THE WAY OF SERVICE

Service to God—Service to Men

By this time we have become familiar with the notion that *yes to God* includes service to God. God "gives orders," and his orders are to be obeyed with "unconditional obedience." In this perspective we have also seen that one additional thing stands firm: service to God can be realized only through service to men, to humanity. This second assertion, however, has its problems, and our principal question now becomes: What is the role of God in relation to this service to men?

For a starting point, let us turn to what Hammarskjöld wrote on Christmas Eve 1955 (p.104). Two passages from that day are important: the first deals with human love; the second begins with the words, "God desires our independence." It will be necessary to see these words in their context. When writing about human love, Hammarskjöld begins by saying: "Two old inklings, the far-reaching significance of which I have only recently perceived." Here we have one of the rare occasions on which Hammarskjöld refers directly to something he has written earlier. One of the two earlier passages which he here has in mind is also a rather extraordinary consideration of human love: "When you have reached the point where you no longer expect a response, you will at last be able to give in such a way that the other is able to receive, and be grateful. When Love has matured and, through a dissolution of the self into light, become a radiance, then shall the Lover be liberated from dependence upon the Beloved, and the Beloved also be made perfect by being liberated from the Lover" (p.78). Here he obviously places strong demands on human love. These demands are even accentuated in the statement of Christmas Eve 1955: "The Lover desires the perfection of the Beloved—which requires, among other things, the liberation of the

Beloved from the Lover" (p. 105'). Then Hammarskjöld leaves the theme of human love and turns instead to the divine love: "God desires our independence—in which we 'fall' back into God when we cease to strive for it ourselves" (p. 105*).

When we have read these two Christmas Eve passages together, our first investigation must be into what Hammarskjöld means when he says that he only recently has perceived "the far-reaching significance" of the earlier entries. It is difficult, perhaps impossible, to give a complete answer. However, one thing seems to be clear: "the far-reaching significance" has reference to what was written about the relation to God. If, perchance, it also refers to human love, the meaning would be that the demand here placed on human love can hardly be satisfied. Be that as it may, the statement about the relation to God is quite unmistakable and can, in fact, appropriately be described as a classic expression of the meaning of Christian faith in God—freedom through self-surrender to God. "God desires our independence"—Christian faith signifies a new freedom; but in this freedom we fall back into God. Dependence on God is the prerequisite to our liberation, our independence, our freedom; and therefore our independence is a gift from God not to be attained by our own efforts to gain it. Thus has Hammarskjöld described what the love of God means to him. Commitment to this power implies liberation and "independence."

This quality of relationship between God and man clearly has far-reaching consequences. First, all moralistic tendencies disappear—for God is no moralist. He does not prescribe in detail what we ought or ought not to do. Independence means that at every point man must decide how to act; every case must be treated according to the demands of the situation; every act must be performed on man's own authority—and therefore man is always responsible for what he does. *Markings* is filled with pronouncements which strongly emphasize this inescapable responsibility —characteristically, for example, in an entry, already quoted in its entirety, in which Hammarskjöld writes of the terrifying responsibility that is his: "If you fail, it is God, thanks to your having betrayed him, who will fail mankind."

This accent on the independence, authority, and responsibility of man might mean that the role of God in man's life of action is of little consequence. Such a conclusion, however, would be foolhardy, for God does not cease giving the orders which are to be obeyed. It is significant, however, that at one point Hammarskjöld writes: "Thy orders are given in secret. May I always hear them—and obey" (p. 125). Chiefly, hearing and obeying mean two things: to act in complete self-surrender and to act in love according to the will of God. These are, of course, inseparably combined: self-surrender is a prerequisite for acting in love.

We have already seen how definite and unreserved the demand for self-surrender is to Hammarskjöld: "One result of 'God's union with the soul' is a union with other people which does not draw back before the ultimate surrender of the self" (p. 137*). But self-surrender is the prior condition for self-realization in action: "You will find that the freedom of the continual farewell, the hourly self-surrender, gives to your experience of reality the purity and clarity which signify—self-realization. You will find that obedience requires an act of will which must continually be reiterated, and that you will fail, if anything in your personal life is allowed to slip back into the center" (p. 114). Here the word *center* means self-centeredness; although *center* in fact can also be used in a quite different sense. In 1957 he wrote: "'The Uncarved Block'—remain at the Center, which is yours and that of human reactions. For those goals which it gives to your life, do the utmost which, at each moment, is possible for you. Also, act without thinking of the consequences, or seeking anything for yourself" (pp. 135-6*). Here Center—spelled with a capital *C*—is a word of honor, representing the opposite of self-centeredness and chaos; it is the power that unites and keeps together; ultimately, it is the love of God.

In light of this, one of the prayers of *Markings*—appearing in various forms—thus centers around this subject: "To love life and men as God loves them—for the sake of their infinite possibilities" (p. 112). In his article "Motivations and Methods of Dag Hammarskjöld" Andrew Cordier recalls a conversation between Hammarskjöld and a prominent scientist in which they discussed the intellectual and spiritual qualities which ought to be brought to bear upon diplomatic negotiations. When the scientist concluded by saying that the whole matter finally came down to the short, simple word *love,* Hammarskjöld was deeply moved; he repeatedly discussed the answer with Cordier.[1] Certainly, no answer could have been more in harmony with Hammarskjöld's own view and his deepest intentions. His conviction that the way of loving service is a combination of self-surrender and self-realization can be summed up in the following very characteristic watchword: "Out of myself as a stumbling block, into myself as fulfillment" (p. 130).

Hammarskjöld's understanding of service can be further illustrated by two statements which treat the subject of *sanctification*. Hammarskjöld gives, we could say, two different definitions of sanctification—two definitions which complement each other. The first appears in the context of a discussion of "the mystical experience": "The 'mystical experience.' Always *here* and *now*—in that freedom which is one with distance, in that stillness which is born of silence. But—this is a freedom in the midst of action, a stillness in the midst of other human beings. The mystery is a constant reality to him who, in this world, is free from self-concern, a reality that grows peaceful and mature before the receptive attention of assent." Then Hammarskjöld continues: "In our era, the road to sanctification necessarily passes through action" (p. 108*).

The second definition of sanctification is to be found in a context already familiar to us. Hammarskjöld in this case makes use of the symbol of light. "You are not the oil, you are not the air—merely the point of combustion, the flash-point where the light is born. You are merely the lens in the beam. You can only receive, give, and possess the light as a lens does. If you seek yourself, 'your rights,' you prevent the oil and air from meeting in the flame, you rob the lens of its transparency." Then the definition follows: "Sanctification—to be the light or in the light, self-effaced so that it may be born, self-effaced so that it may be focused and spread wider" (p. 133*). It must be noted that the original Swedish in both of these passages uses the same theological term, which is properly translated as *sanctification;* the English uses *holiness* in the first instance, *sanctity* in the second, but neither of these expressions is adequate to the technical word used by Hammarskjöld.

---

[1] Andrew W. Cordier, "Motivations and Methods of Dag Hammarskjöld," in *Paths to World Order,* ed. Andrew W. Cordier and Kenneth Maxwell (New York: Columbia University Press, 1967), p. 3.

These two passages require analysis. The first, a very remarkable entry, appears in a context which is by no means surprising—Hammarskjöld's characteristic connection between the "mystical experience" and the service of men. The "mystical experience" involves openness towards the world and its manifold troubles; the freedom given in this experience is a "freedom in the midst of action." The subsequent definition of action, however, is unusual and striking. The first words are immediately significant: "In our era." Day and night throughout the years Hammarskjöld dealt with the world's problems, but very seldom does *Markings* refer directly to "our era." Only rarely does he use an expression such as "modern man"—one of those infrequent occasions is his radio address of 1953 in which he says that Schweitzer provided a "key for modern man to the world of the Gospels," accentuating the importance of historico-critical investigations for our relation to and understanding of the biblical message. In the present instance, his mention of "our era" in connection with "sanctification" obviously implies that "our era" presents a unique requirement for "sanctification."

The background of Hammarskjöld's statement is, of course, to be found in traditional convictions about faith and its fruits: no faith apart from works; faith without deeds is dead. But such general Christian pronouncements do not disclose everything that Hammarskjöld has in mind when he asserts that in the present situation the road to sanctification necessarily passes through action. This is not a traditional combination, and in order adequately to interpret it we must consider two of Hammarskjöld's main ideas while also bearing in mind the worldwide perspective required in his position at the United Nations.

First, then, is his central theme concerning the contrast between creation and destruction, between the creative and the destructive powers of existence. The question that Hammarskjöld here asks of himself is the same we have met before in considering his "ordeal-by-fire": "Do you create? Or destroy?" Ultimately, to create means to be an instrument of the only power authentically creative—the love of God. To be sure, Hammarskjöld does not hold that actions of this kind are a uniquely Christian prerogative. His outlook towards non-Christian religions clearly requires him to draw no limits around the love of God and its possibilities. Faith in God, being in his hands, always includes the inescapable duty to serve his creating will of love. Second is Hammarskjöld's strong emphasis on the *imitatio Christi,* the imitation of Christ through sacrifice "for the sake of others." This way of self-surrendering sacrifice is the road to sanctification which passes through action.

Behind all such considerations looms Hammarskjöld's own situation. His main concern at the United Nations was the peace of the world, an incredibly complicated and demanding concern. He made the office of the Secretary General of the United Nations into a position of pivotal significance for all mankind. Hammarskjöld's speeches and statements, collected by Wilder Foote in *Servant of Peace,*[2] ought to be read as a commentary on his affirmations concerning the necessary combination of sanctification and action. The actions which Dag Hammarskjöld felt were required "in our era" were not only works of mercy, what we usually call "good works." What our situation demands is the action of righteousness. Indeed, *righteousness* is a key word in all of Hammarskjöld's statements.

Hammarskjöld did not live to the era of the Second Vatican Council and the crucial recent assemblies of the World Council of Churches which have emphasized so strongly the church's responsibilities in relation to the world and its manifold problems. These events and the attitude behind them may well one day be viewed as a turning point in church history. Hammarskjöld's assertion that the road to sanctification passes through action is an eloquent testimony to the driving force of his career and, indeed, to much of the most creative concern which men are today showing for their world.

Let us now deal more briefly with Hammarskjöld's second definition of sanctification. His view is in two directions: outward to actions which are to be seen as trials and ordeals, and inward to the spiritual life. But these two perspectives belong intimately together. It is, as we have seen, impossible to speak of actions on the road to sanctification in Hammarskjöld's sense without considering the sacrifice which is required. Sanctification belongs to the inner life as a prerequisite to the sanctification which appears in the trials and ordeals of action.

The content of this second definition is already familiar to us. We

---

[2] Wilder Foote, ed., *Servant of Peace: A Selection of the Speeches and Statements of Dag Hammarskjöld* (New York: Harper, 1962).

remember that Hammarskjöld in an almost biblical way uses the word *light* as a chief symbol for the love of God or, on occasion, the Spirit of God. No human light is self-resplendent. Sanctification means to be transparent to the divine light—man can only be the "lens" through which the light shines. Every tendency to self-centeredness robs the lens of its transparency. Self-effacement, therefore, is a condition antecedent to the transparency of the lens. Then—and only then—to be sanctified is to "be the light or in the light." Thus sanctification is not a gift to be possessed and kept for one's own use. Its purpose is to allow the light to be focused and *spread wider*. In other words, sanctification is to result in actions of love and righteousness, such as are required "in our era."

The main concern of this chapter is the action of service. We have heard Hammarskjöld say that God wills our independence—and thus from one point of view actions are to be performed in freedom, on our own authority, and on our own responsibility, our freedom even being a "freedom to betray God." At the same time God gives and, still more, he is the God who acts through human instruments. The light of God's love is thus revealed in men's actions. The juxtaposition of these aspects is further elucidated by certain sections of *Markings* which deal with the relation between the actions of God and the actions of men. Hammarskjöld's central theme is that all creative and constructive actions have their origin in God and, ultimately, are his own works.

Hammarskjöld makes important use of two quotations from Sir Thomas Browne's *Religio Medici:* "I cannot go to cure the body of my patient, but I forget my profession, and call unto God for his soul"; and "We carry with us the wonders we seek without us." Hammarskjöld evaluates these as "sayings resonant with significance—to one who is seeking the Kingdom of God, they contain the truth about *all* work" (p. 118). As so often in *Markings,* two different perspectives here complement each other. There are situations in which man can do nothing other than resign everything to God—in prayer. There are other situations, however, in which we carry with us the power to do "wonders," a power given to man by the God who himself "does wonders." Hammarskjöld had earlier taken up this theme in a reference to Psalm 77:14: "Thou art the God that doest wonders: and hast declared thy power among the peoples" (p. 103). The theme returns again later: "We act in faith—and wonders occur. In consequence, we are tempted to make the wonders the ground for our faith. The cost of such weakness is that we lose the confidence of faith" (p. 125*). (The Swedish word *under* can also be translated "miracle," as in the English translation of *Markings*.)

The two quotations from Browne are crucial. Hammarskjöld asserts that, to one who is seeking the kingdom of God, they contain the truth about *all* work. He may here have had in mind the exhortation of the Sermon on the Mount to seek first the kingdom of God and the freedom from anxiety promised with that exhortation. Hammarskjöld, in fact, more than once quotes the latter promise (Matt. 6:31–33). In any case, something of this freedom from anxiety is to be found in Hammarskjöld's interpretation of Browne. Whether man must confess his complete incompetence or whether he possesses the capability of working wonders, the confidence that the kingdom of God will be realized does not fail—He is "confident of victory" (p. 92).

In this connection, two quotations from Meister Eckhart are also important; both deal with the kingdom of God. Again we meet a juxtaposition of two different perspectives which seem to complement each other. In the first quotation it is held that works done according to the law of God's kingdom leave men "undisturbed." Hammarskjöld italicized the last of Eckhart's words: *"For works neither give them anything, nor take anything from them"* (p. 138). These words seem to say that life in union with God is not dependent on works; in the kingdom of God there is no merit in works, nor do works "disturb" life with God. And again, Eckhart: " 'In the Kingdom of God'— ; —all works are equal there, my smallest is as my greatest, my greatest as my smallest.— About works in themselves there is something divisive which causes a division in the souls of men, and brings them to the brink of disquiet" (p. 138). *Markings* more than once emphasizes the impossibility of distinguishing between great and small works. That works "in themselves" bring souls of men to the brink of disquiet certainly was a notion familiar to Hammarskjöld.

Nevertheless, Hammarskjöld does not use the idea—that the question of success or failure, and of the value of work, must be left to God, and that men must be indifferent and "undisturbed" about the results of their actions—in quite the same way as Eckhart. At two noteworthy points we can see how Hammarskjöld considers questions of this kind. The first concerns his attitude towards successes: "To rejoice at a success is not the same as taking credit for it. To deny oneself the first is to become a hypocrite and a denier of life; to permit oneself the second is a childish indulgence which will prevent one from ever growing up" (p. 113). Man never has cause to boast. Further: "God sometimes gives us the honor—for His work. Or withdraws from it into His solitude: He watches our capers on the stage with an ironic smile—so long as we do not tamper with the scales of justice" (p. 98 *). A refrain, more than once sounded in *Markings*, is the first verse of Psalm 115: "Not unto us, O Lord, but unto thy name give the praise . . ." (p. 99).

Finally, Hammarskjöld's decisive word about the relation between the acts of God and the acts of man appears after his definition of sanctification as self-effacement in the light: "You will know Life and be acknowledged by it according to your degree of transparency, your capacity, that is, to vanish as an end, and remain purely as a means" (p. 133). If man is only an instrument, then, in the obedience and light of union with God, each act is "an act of creation, conscious, because you are a human being with human responsibilities, but governed, nevertheless, by the power beyond human consciousness which has created man" (p. 139). Ultimately the way of action is to be seen in the perspective of God's continuous, creative activity—which will continue until the kingdom of God is realized.

"Dedicated"

In 1952 Hammarskjöld wrote: "Pray that your loneliness may spur you into finding something to live for, great enough to die for" (p. 85). No spur was necessary, for his wishes were fulfilled with no special effort on his part. Quite unexpectedly he received a special and very extraordinary assignment, one which readily aroused a deep sense of "dedication." We have already referred to his immediate reactions to the appointment to the United Nations: in conversation with a friend and in certain writings on the occasion of his departure for America. At the time of that departure he had as yet had no experience of what it meant to be Secretary General of the United Nations. What did he think of his task during the years of action in New York?

Let us first listen to two entries in *Markings* from 1955, both most revealing of his attitude to his calling: " 'Thine . . .' A sacrifice—and a liberation—to obey a will for which 'I' is in no respect a goal! 'Dedicated . . .' A reward—or a price— to be committed to a task in comparison with which nothing I could seek for myself is of any value" (p. 98 *). The words *Thine* and *dedicated* (or *consecrated,* but not *destined,* as in the English translation) show how Hammarskjöld related his vocation to God, in consequence of which he, as always, felt a complete self-surrender which was simultaneously a liberation. The same strong feeling of having been dedicated returns in the second entry, where we also catch a glimpse of how he looked at the United Nations: "You are dedicated to this task—as the sacrifice in a still barbarian cult, because of the divine intention behind it: a feeble creation of men's hands—but you have to give your all to this human dream for the sake of that which alone gives it reality" (p. 100*). It ought not to surprise us that Hammarskjöld speaks of sacrifice in connection with his task. More surprising is his reference to "a barbarian cult." The sense of the passage seems to be that even as—in spite of everything—the divine "intention" stands behind that which seems to be only "a barbarian cult," just so a "human dream" is working in that which seems to be only "a feeble creation of men's hands." This dream would be nothing but a dream if it had no root in the feeble human creation; therefore Hammarskjöld gives his all to the dream by working for the feeble creation. It ought only to be added that Hammarskjöld undoubtedly held that the human dream emanated from "the divine intention." Two years later, in the midst of his term as Secretary General, his attitude towards his vocation is unchanged, but perhaps an attentive ear can hear something of a new tune: an exhortation not to complain. "For someone whose job so obviously mirrors man's extraordinary possibilities and responsibilities, there is no excuse if he loses his sense of 'having been called.' So long as he keeps that, everything he can do has a meaning, nothing a price. Therefore: if he complains, he is accusing—himself" (p. 132).

Hammarskjöld's view that the United Nations is a feeble creation of man's hands is elaborated in *Markings:* a feeble creation, yes—but at the same time the greatest creation of mankind: "A jealous dream which refuses to share you with anybody or anything else: the greatest creation of mankind—the dream of mankind. The greatest creation of mankind, in which it is the noblest dream of the individual—to lose himself. Therefore: gladly death or humiliation if that is what the dream demands" (p. 103). At another point Hammarskjöld explains the contrast between the weakness of the organization and the greatness of its aim. In the light of this contrast, the responsibility of his service is accentuated: "It is an *idea* you are serving—an idea which must be victorious if a mankind worth the name is to survive. It is this idea which you must help towards victory with all your strength—not the work of human hands which just now gives you responsibility and the responsibility-creating chance to further it" (p. 119).

Whenever Hammarskjöld considered the nature of his task, he seemed to concentrate on his responsibility; in fact, his considerations can well be described as an explanation of the biblical words, "Every one to whom much is given, of him will much be required" (Luke 12:48). The greatness of his task could not be denied. But this was nothing to boast of; it only demanded greater responsibility. Hammarskjöld did not consider his work more elevated than that of others. Characteristically, he writes: "How poor is the courage which knows its 'why,' compared to the quiet heroism an unreflective mind can display in the most inglorious and degrading trials. How favored by the gods is he, whose character is tested in situations where courage has a meaning for him—perhaps, even, a tangible reward. How little does he know about his potential weakness, how easily may he be trapped and blinded by self-admiration" (p. 115). Hammarskjöld returns often to this theme: the decisive thing is how a man acts, not the external conditions of his life: "You will find that, thus subordinated, your life will receive from Life all its meaning, irrespective of the conditions given you for its realization" (p. 114). Ultimately, the decisive question is the question of love. In a rather long statement which begins by asserting that the "great commitment" all too easily obscures the "little," Hammarskjöld writes: "Love . . . would remain a sublime sort of superhuman self-assertion, powerless against the negative forces within you, if it were not tamed by the yoke of human intimacy and warmed by its tenderness. It is better for the health of the soul to make one man good than 'to sacrifice oneself for mankind.' For a mature man, these are not alternatives, but two aspects of self-realization, which mutually support each other, both being the outcome of one and the same choice" (p. 116).

In comparing his task to others, Hammarskjöld found it humiliating to consider the courage and sacrifice, the high ethical standards to be found "in the most inglorious and degrading trials." He felt his own task a privileged one, and such comparisons gave rise to utterances like the one on his birthday in 1958: "How incredibly great is what I have been given, and how meaningless what I have to 'sacrifice' " (p. 140). On the other hand, he knew only too well that the diplomacy and political affairs which comprised his task had their own particular and dangerous ethical difficulties. He writes: "The most dangerous of all moral dilemmas [literally: The most dangerous lesson]: when we are obliged to conceal truth in order to help the truth to be victorious. If this should at any time become our duty in the role assigned us by destiny, how strait must be our path at all times if we are not to perish" (p. 127*). Here we see clearly not only those things which Hammarskjöld considered to be risky though inevitable difficulties in politics but also his own carefulness and conscientiousness in performing his duties.

When we survey Hammarskjöld's years as Secretary General, do we observe any changes in his attitude to his task and work? In the main, certainly, his attitude remained the same during these years; always we find the same strong feeling of responsibility and the same thankfulness for the task entrusted to him. An entry in *Markings* on New Year's Eve 1956 can be considered his password: "Gratitude and readiness. You got all for nothing. Do not hesitate, when it is asked for, to give your all, which, in fact, is nothing, for all" (p.126). His penchant for self-criticism is always present. He frequently records a shortcoming or failure of his own, and always he approaches God with gratitude whenever a step towards the peace of humanity seems to have been taken. Ultimately, he considered all good work as a work of God himself; man was only an instrumentality. On Christmas Eve 1956 he wrote in typical fashion: "Your own efforts 'did not bring it to pass,' only God—but rejoice if God found a use for your efforts in His work. Rejoice if you feel that what you did was 'necessary,' but remember, even so, that you were simply the instrument by means of which He added one tiny grain to the wholeness He has created for His own purposes" (p. 123*).

There are, however, points in *Markings* which reflect how deeply Hammarskjöld could be depressed by the intrigues, power struggles, and chicanery characteristic of much of the world of politics. He wrote with candor: "Living submerged in this heavy *Fluidum* of the sub-human—sub-human in insight, feeling, and energy—beware of a twofold danger—of drowning and of floating—of lowering yourself until this position below the clear surface of the truly human seems to you the natural one, and of upholding your banner in a vacuum of 'superiority.' The fact is that, in this position, 'love and patience, righteousness and humility,' are necessary even for your own peace and comfort" (p. 121). Doubtless, he at times did find it difficult to locate the "spark" that, according to his view of man, ought to be present everywhere. He fought, not least in his prayers, against every tendency towards contempt of others. He knew that "the man who 'likes people' disposes once and for all of the man who despises them" (p. 102). An aim of prayer is "to love life and men as God loves them" (p. 112), and a central demand of the proper imitation of Christ is to live "with the humility of Him who has suffered all the possibilities of betrayal" (p. 118). In spite of his deepest convictions and confidence, however, it cannot be denied that Hammarskjöld's view of man took on darker shades during his last years.

Utterances like the one about the "heavy *Fluidum*" are very rare in *Markings*. It may indeed be correct to combine them with the tiredness which shows itself in the "Road Marks" of Hammarskjöld's last years. In fact, the first entry that speaks directly of fatigue—some verses from October 1958—also speaks of "intrigues":

> Words without import
> Are lobbed to and fro
> Between us.
>
> Forgotten intrigues
> With their spider's web
> Snare our hands.

"DEDICATED"

> Choked by its clown's mask
> And quite dry, my mind
> Is crumbling. (p. 142.)

And a week later Hammarskjöld writes the following melancholy lines: "Too tired for company, / You seek a solitude / You are too tired to fill" (p. 146). Certainly, he had an enormous capacity for work, but, as is well known, he was often required to work day and night with a minimum of rest. The most expressive description of his tiredness he committed to paper in June 1961:

> Tired
> And lonely,
> So tired
> The heart aches.
> Meltwater trickles
> Down the rocks,
> The fingers are numb,
> The knees tremble.
> It is now,
> Now, that you must not give in.
>
> On the path of the others
> Are resting places,
> Places in the sun
> Where they can meet.
> But this
> Is your path,
> And it is now,
> Now, that you must not fail.
>
> Weep
> If you can,
> Weep,
> But do not complain.
> The way chose you—
> And you must be thankful. (p. 175.)

THE WAY OF SERVICE

Hammarskjöld's words from 1952 ring on: "something to live for, great enough to die for." *Markings* shows that his thoughts often moved towards the subject of death. During his years of crisis suicide could even appear enticing—as a temptation, however, that must without hesitation be rejected as treachery. There are no indications that he necessarily feared death; he had always known that the task entrusted to him involved sacrifice. In his last years he increasingly emphasized the premonition that the sacrifice could or would be a sacrifice of death. At the end of 1957 we find a series of five entries in *Markings,* all of them dealing with death. The first runs: "Do not seek death. Death will find you. But seek the road which makes death a fulfillment." The second asserts that the body "must become familiar with its death . . . as a self-evident, imminent, and emotionally neutral step on the way towards the goal you have found worthy of your life." The third accentuates the fact that death ought not to be embellished: "As an element in the sacrifice, death is a fulfillment, but more often it is a degradation, and it is never an elevation." The fourth speaks about two abysses to be avoided: "The *arête* that leads to the summit separates two abysses: the pleasure-tinged death wish . . . and the animal fear . . . . Only he can conquer vertigo, whose body has learned to treat itself as a means" (p. 136). The fifth entry, already quoted and discussed,[3] stresses the necessity of always being prepared for death.

It is impossible not to read Hammarskjöld's later writings about death as a gloomy omen of what was soon to happen. But Hammarskjöld did not write in that frame of mind. These passages do not exhibit anxiety, nervousness, or hesitation. At the end of 1959 he writes: "That chapter [literally: The balancing] is closed. / Nothing binds me: / All is made ready, all waiting" (p. 160). In one of the verses, dated July 7, 1960–Spring 1961, we read:

> Asked if I have courage
> To go on to the end,
> I answer Yes without
> A second thought. (p. 170)

---

[3] See p. 79 above, the quotation from p. 160 of *Markings.*

"DEDICATED"

In June 1961 he states quite calmly: "Others have gone before, others will follow." The verse immediately preceding runs:

> What have I to fear?
> If their arrows hit,
> If their arrows kill,
> What is there in that
> To cry about? (p. 172.)

His firmness of mind he evidenced in these lines: "For him who has faith, / The last miracle / Shall be greater than the first" (p. 162).

Here we may have reason to take into consideration two utterances which in the Swedish original are directly combined with the passage written on Easter of 1960.[4] Hammarskjöld writes: "When I think of those who have preceded me, I feel as if I were at a party in the dead hour which has to be got through after the Guests of Honor have left." "When I think of those who will come after—or survive me—I feel as if I were taking part in the preparations for a feast, the joys of which I shall not share" (p. 163). Some commentators have correctly said that there is nothing of Easter joy in these sentences. The first utterance seems strange. It is difficult to know who the "Guests of Honor" are, for Hammarskjöld obviously does not think highly of the spiritual level of the contemporary generation. However, it is the second sentence which is really surprising: his very hopeful look towards the future. Such words could hardly have been written by a gloomy and depressed mind.

I shall conclude this examination of Hammarskjöld's outlook at the end of his years by quoting some brief verses from 1960 which bear witness to the heaviness of his burden and the strength of his soul. No words could be more illuminating.

> The road,
> You shall follow it.
>
> The fun,
> You shall forget it.

---

[4] See pp. 85–88 above and pp. 129–30 below.

THE WAY OF SERVICE

The cup,
You shall empty it.

The pain,
You shall conceal it.

The truth,
You shall be told it.

The end,
You shall endure it. (p. 167.)

Chapter Six

RETROSPECTIVE SURVEY

Was Hammarskjöld a Mystic?

That Dag Hammarskjöld in *Markings* frequently quotes both the Bible and certain important contemporary poets is not surprising. One expects a diary which reveals struggles such as those which occupied Hammarskjöld also to present a deep grasp of biblical questions and affirmations. Furthermore, we know that Hammarskjöld was at home in the land of the muses; he had made a mark as a translator of St. John Pérse from French to Swedish.

To many readers, however, it is surprising that *Markings* is so dependent upon the medieval mystics. The author of the book quotes them frequently—especially Meister Eckhart and Thomas à Kempis—and furthermore the insights and even the language of these figures leave distinct traces in Hammarskjöld's own writings. It seems reasonable, therefore, to put the question: Was Hammarskjöld himself a mystic?

Mysticism is a word to be used only with hesitation and attentive carefulness. It is one of the most ambiguous words in the vocabulary of religion and theology; different definitions of mysticism are innumerable, some being so vague as to say nothing, others being so precise as to exclude almost everything. In the first case, mysticism expands beyond all limits and becomes nearly synonymous with religion as such; in the second case, the limits of mysticism's dominion are reduced to the point where it becomes an extremely rare experience and a matter only for specialized research.

The same ambiguity is to be found when the question of the relation between mysticism and Christian faith is faced. There are those who attempt to make "faith" and "mysticism" categories as distinct from each other as possible; and there are those who more or less identify mysticism with *the* authentic Christian faith. For instance, when mysticism is described as communion with God, as a relation of intimate confidence to be realized here and now, and when mysticism is held to affirm that all statements about God are symbolic and that behind every human understanding of God there is always inexplicable mystery—then in fact mysticism has been described with words which belong just as clearly to any living, conscious Christian faith. A faith deprived of these features would be nothing but a caricature. It must be remembered that among many in this century *mysticism* has been and still is a fashionable word and a designation of honor. It has very often been esteemed a religious attitude of higher quality than "ordinary" Christian faith. Thus it is that many speak and write of mysticism quite innocently, without the slightest awareness of all the complications connected with the term.

In light of the very ambiguity of the term, therefore, the question whether Hammarskjöld is to be designated a mystic cannot be answered by a simple yes or no. The important thing for us, accordingly, is not to decide whether he was a mystic or not, but to ferret out what the mystics meant for him. He has himself clearly informed us that the mystics important to him were "the great medieval mystics," and he has also explicitly said that the help they gave led to a better understanding of the Christian faith. We have considered this subject in the foregoing chapters, and there is no need to repeat here what has already been said. In this concluding chapter, however, certain very general remarks concerning the problem of mysticism in *Markings* are appropriate.

It is hardly surprising that the relation between mysticism and Christian faith must be described as double-sided. There is, on the one hand, not the slightest doubt that in the course of history movements of "mysticism" have been sources of life-giving power for Christians. Such movements have on more than one occasion revitalized central aspects of Christian faith that had been partially or completely suppressed. Mysticism has, for example, always emphasized the life with God as the center of faith, thus correcting other one-sided and narrow conceptions of faith. Books of devotion such as Thomas à Kempis's *Imitatio Christi,* frequently used by Hammarskjöld, have served through the centuries as valuable spiritual guides.

On the other hand, however, it cannot be denied that mysticism has at times caused an erosion of Christian faith. The "inwardness" or introspective concern of mysticism can lead to a very self-centered piety. Its accent on the "immediate" relationship to God can disengage mysticism from the anchorage in history which characterizes Christian faith. Its emphasis on finding God in the "wholeness," in the totality of existence, can lead to a pantheistic view and, via pantheism, to an "atheism": everywhere becomes nowhere.

This double-sided influence of mysticism is manifest in the history of the Middle Ages. The medieval mystics who meant so much to Hammarskjöld no doubt in many ways acted as a positive and creative force for the faith of that period. But it is not difficult to discover, especially in the later part of the Middle Ages, offshoots of mysticism which, in the manner we have described, did lead away from Christian faith. Similar developments have occurred, not only in the Middle Ages, but in all eras of Christian history. In our own day, even, there has been talk of a revival of mysticism; in fact, it is not difficult to discover in modern literature this double-sided influence of "mysticism."

For Hammarskjold, mysticism doubtless provided a way forward into Christian faith. The last words in his radio address of 1953 are significant. Talking about "the great medieval mystics," he concludes: "I know that their discoveries about the laws of inner life and of action have not lost their significance."[1] Obviously, this indicates that Hammarskjöld did not consider the help he had received from the mystics a support to be dismissed from mind and sight once it had accomplished its work. On the contrary, the discoveries of the mystics contained essential values worth contemplation and use even in our time. When Hammarskjöld speaks of "discoveries," he has in mind not only "the inner life" and "action" but also the relation between these two aspects, the "laws" which are in operation here.

We have seen that Hammarskjöld interpreted the mystics very much in his own way. He approached them with his own very precise and definite preconceptions and anticipations. Most striking, perhaps, is his emphasis on the role of action in the medieval mystics. Hammarskjöld himself never doubted that life ought to be used in the service of others, in action, and with that certainty as a starting point he found exactly

---

[1] Dag Hammarskjöld, "Old Creeds in a New World," in *Servant of Peace,* ed. Wilder Foote (New York: Harper, 1962), p. 24.

what he was seeking in the "great medieval mystics." This judgment might be one-sided, but it is not false. Certainly there is any number of statements about the necessity of action in the writings of the mystics appreciated by Hammarskjöld—not only in Thomas à Kempis but also in Meister Eckhart. We can, for instance, call attention to Eckhart's well-known interpretation of the biblical story of Mary and Martha (Luke 10:38–42). According to Eckhart, Martha represents a higher stage than any yet attained by Mary: Mary ought, he says, first to become Martha before she truly can be Mary; she is still in school "to learn life." Eckhart adds: It is better to give food to a hungry man than to remain in enchantment. If a man is in rapture and at the same time knows about a sick person in need of soup, then it is much better in love to leave the rapture and, in greater love, serve the needy.[2]

When Hammarskjöld, pointing to the mystics, speaks about the *inner life,* he often describes this life as God's union with the soul. "The inner life" thus becomes synonymous with faith. The oft-repeated words of Saint John of the Cross, "Faith is God's union with the soul," is a determination he has found to illuminate the real character of faith. In other words, faith means an existential relation to God. Hammarskjöld thus found the description by the medieval mystics of the meaning of the inner life fresh and unconventional; it was a message which disclosed new and essential insights. Again, it must be remembered that in some way he was prepared to receive just that kind of liberating message. Even in his early writings we meet more than once the notion that faith in God must be something more than an intellectual assent to God's existence or to doctrines about him; it must also be something more than a special kind of human "feeling." During 1941–42 he wrote, "When we are compelled to look ourselves in the face—then He rises above us in terrifying reality, beyond all argument and 'feeling,' stronger than all self-defensive forgetfulness" (p. 57). Even if, at that time, he did not acknowledge any faith in God, he was nevertheless quite aware that such faith required an existential relation.

[2] Otto Karrer, *Meister Eckhart: Das System seiner religiösen Lehre und Lebensweisheit* (Munich, 1926), p. 190. Cf. Ray C. Petry, ed., *Late Medieval Mysticism,* Library of Christian Classics, vol. 8 (Philadelphia: Westminster, 1957), pp. 193–99, 207, 179.

We have called attention to the fact that in the history of Christianity mysticism has often acted as a corrective. Such a statement can be certified by reference to Hammarskjöld. What he "discovered" in his contact with the medieval mystics acted as a corrective to an intellectualistic conception of faith. Even more, it operated as a corrective to a one-sided ethical conception of the Christian life. We must not forget Hammarskjöld's *but,* when, in his radio address of 1953, he turned from Albert Schweitzer to the medieval mystics. It seems that he interpreted Schweitzer as one who more or less identified the stream of love which appears in human life with God or the divine element. In the mystics' explanations of "the inner life," however, God was in his own being purely the center, the all-dominating power. And Hammarskjöld's yes was ultimately a yes to a God on whom all that belonged to the inner life—and to the whole of life—was dependent. This did not mean a reduced accent on ethics and action, but it meant that life received a new center —and *Markings* bears consistent witness to that fact. It can hardly be denied that the mystics were a factor of importance during the time when Hammarskjöld's yes to God was growing in secret. We also know well that their influence was not limited to that period of his life.

But did this influence remain constant throughout the years? Most of the quotations from the mystics were recorded in 1955 and 1956. Before that time there were very few quotations, and in the years 1957 and 1958 the last quotations appeared, one in each year. These statistics seemingly indicate that the influence of the mystics reached its height in the mid-fifties. However, such a conclusion would be too hasty, for in the years after 1958 we find in Hammarskjöld's own entries terms and formulas which are clear indications of the enduring influence of the mystics. Throughout 1959 we encounter in the prose entries expressions of this sort: "In 'faith'—an unbroken living contact with all things. . . . The self . . . *is*—is nothing, yet at the same time one with everything. . . . Simplicity [in the English translation: To have humility] is to experience reality, not *in relation to ourselves,* but in its sacred independence" (pp. 147–8*). Most of the entries from 1960 and 1961 are poems and prayers, both of a very intimate, personal character; the only entries written in prose are those from Easter and Christmas Eve, which we have discussed,[3] and the summary statement of Whitsunday 1961, which speaks only of God and Christ. Even if in these two last years we do not find direct reference to the mystics, it must nevertheless be said that in general the influence of the mystics remains a component part of *Markings*.

As a concluding—and summarizing—thesis for this book's examination of Hammarskjöld's relation to mysticism, I should like to offer the statement, already obvious, that that relation must be understood as a *dialectical* one. The writings of the mystics themselves are, certainly, complicated and dialectical; our intention, however, is not to examine the mystics but to offer an understanding of Hammarskjöld's relation to them—and for that the rubric *dialectical* is most appropriate.

In this examination we note first of all that some of Hammarskjöld's expressions which seem to affirm mysticism are balanced by views which not only expose limits and potentially extreme conclusions, but even point in opposite directions, thus simultaneously correcting and completing the original statements. It might, for example, be significant that Hammarskjöld, when introducing the expression *the "mystical experience"* (p. 108), places these words within quotation marks and thus seems to indicate caution with regard to the expression. He is cautious, of course, towards that which is usually called the mystical experience but which he elsewhere describes with the simple word *faith*.

In the history of mysticism it is possible to discern representative elements that seem to bind different figures, eras, or even "schools" together. One such element is the important role that introspection plays in mysticism; another is the custom of speaking of God in abstract terms, such as *oneness* and *wholeness*, and of considering union with God as submergence in the divine wholeness. There are utterances in *Markings* that have—or seem to have—affinity to these two elements typical of the mystics.

In considering introspection we notice formulas such as "descend into yourself and encounter the Other" (p. 139); "the point of rest at the center of our being"; "to see, judge and act from the point of rest in

---

[3] See pp. 85–88 above and pp. 129–30 below; pp. 83–84 above.

ourselves" (p. 148). Such pronouncements are clearly not vague phrases; they mean much to Hammarskjöld. They assert primarily that a relation to God is not merely a relation to a past event or to a future hope; it is rather an immediate contact in man's inner life here and now. When you descend into yourself and meet the Other, then, Hammarskjöld continues, "do you . . . experience goodness as the ultimate reality—united and living—*in* Him and *through* you" (p. 139). In the immediately preceeding passage Hammarskjöld gives a more exact explanation of the *how* of this contact. He has spoken about faith as a union with God, and he continues, "With this faith, in *prayer* [italics mine] you descend into yourself to meet the Other" (p. 139). Immediate contact with God is a contact realized in and through prayer. Prayer is hardly the exclusive property of mysticism; nor, therefore, is an immediate contact with God.

When Hammarskjöld speaks of resting in the center of our being and acting from "the point of rest in ourselves," he is using expressions which have a quite precise meaning. What he has in mind stands in direct opposition to self-centeredness and self-sufficiency. The "center" of which he speaks can be realized only through relationship with God, through "union" with him. Without such a relation man loses his identity and becomes "chaos": "The chaos you become whenever God's hand does not rest upon your head" (p. 95). To be related to God involves a complete self-surrender that at the same time is self-realization and integrity. Such language is, no doubt, "dialectical" in a way similar to that of the Bible's assertion that life is found by being lost. Hammarskjöld's position is as remote as possible from the self-centered and self-isolating piety which has marked much "mysticism." His faith in God demands realization in action: "In our era, the road to sanctification necessarily passes through action" (p. 108*). But this strong accent on action he combines with a similar emphasis on stillness and silence, terms familiar to the mystics. Such quietness does not call only for a pause in a life overspent with work; it calls for constant, restful communion with God in order to find strength.

As we have seen, Hammarskjöld often refers to God in terms drawn from the mystics: God is Oneness, Unity, Wholeness. Are these terms also to be understood dialectically? In our analysis of the image of God in Chapter Four we observed that, according to Hammarskjöld, the use of these terms was actually an affirmation that existence is meaningful: God is to be found everywhere, making it possible to live in harmony with existence as a whole. As regards this positive view of existence, of creation, let us listen to two successive statements from 1955. In order to prevent misunderstanding of these statements, we should point out that preceding them is a passage—according to the Swedish edition of *Markings,* a quotation written in French—which emphasizes the distance between "the creature and the Creator, time and eternity." Our first statement, which immediately follows this passage, is one of the brightest to be found in Hammarskjöld's diary—remarkably poetic: "Thou takest the pen—and the lines dance. Thou takest the flute—and the notes shimmer. Thou takest the brush—and the colors sing. So all things have meaning and beauty in that space beyond time where Thou art. How, then, can I hold back anything from Thee" (p. 105).

The second statement occupies an exceptional position in *Markings.* At no other point does Hammarskjöld draw so near to the idea of actual submergence in God. The passage describes a vision, a "dream"—the same word that Hammarskjöld used when he spoke about the idea of the United Nations. We ought not, however, to consider the "dream" as only a phantasm; it is, rather, like the needle of a compass which wavers even as it indicates a definite direction. "In a dream I walked with God through the deep places of creation; past walls that receded and gates that opened, through hall after hall of silence, darkness and refreshment—the dwelling place of souls acquainted with light and warmth—until, around me, was an infinity into which we all flowed together and lived anew, like the rings made by raindrops falling upon wide expanses of calm dark waters" (p. 105). We might justifiably use poetic metaphors to describe the "dream"—as a kind of compass needle, or as a window opened towards wide vistas—but we would be seriously in error if we attempted to translate the dream into fixed theological formulas.

Nevertheless, the view of existence which uses the language of the mystics and which appears in statements like the ones we have just considered does not represent all that Hammarskjöld has to say. He has seen existence in the light of God as "the ultimate reality," but he is

WAS HAMMARSKJÖLD A MYSTIC?

very much aware of the fact that existence must also be seen from the point of view of another "reality"—"the reality of evil" (p. 147). His constant and intensely ruthless self-criticism reveals how his piercing eye discovered evil even in hidden places; he had no tendency to idealize existence. Evil is clearly a major preoccupation of *Markings*. The decisive contrast in existence is between the creative power of God and the destructive forces which work in mankind: "Do you create? Or destroy?"

How do these two views of existence coexist? One thing to be carefully noted is that there is no trace of theodicy in *Markings*. There is no accusation against God, and not the slightest hint of a defense of God—such enterprises Hammarskjöld would probably have dismissed as absurd or even blasphemous. The only answer to the question is to be found in the following pregnant words: "Thou who has created us free, Who seest all that happens—yet art confident of victory" (p. 92). God "has created us free"—this involves, as Hammarskjöld once said, a freedom to betray God, but it does not authorize any subsequent accusations against him; God is one "Who seest all that happens"—the reality of evil is not hidden—'yet art confident of victory"—from the perspective of man, the ultimate wonder.

Existence, in this view, must be seen in terms of drama. These terms give to Christ and man's relationship to him a decisive weight; *imitatio* and sacrifice become active words of central importance, culminating in sacrifice as a dynamic, "creative power." As our earlier investigations have shown, this sense of divine and human activity or drama results in a rich and multicolored picture of the image of God and his love. Thus when Hammarskjöld speaks, as the mystics, of God as oneness, wholeness, or unity, he is not describing him as an unqualified entity. On the contrary, these references also carry with them the view of God as "the ultimate reality," that is, as "goodness." In the final analysis, it is the image of God that appears in Christ which utters the decisive word about the divine love, victoriously manifested in sacrifice.

Hammarskjöld does not freeze these visions in ironbound categories, and he is even less interested in confessional formulas. Again and again throughout *Markings* he emphasizes that *mystery* is to be the last word about God. In one of the last pages of the book he writes:

> Thou
> Whom I do not know
> But Whose I am.
> Thou
> Whom I do not comprehend
> But Who hast dedicated me
> To my destiny.
> Thou— (p. 176)

Nevertheless, it is possible, I think, generally to characterize this mystery. *Markings* seems consistently to view it in connection with the love of God, "victorious," "the ultimate reality."

It seems likely that from the mystics of the Middle Ages Hammarskjöld learned to strengthen his accent on mystery. However—once again—to speak of God as mystery, hidden and incomprehensible, is hardly the exclusive right of mysticism. It is an outlook that again and again appears in great Christian thinkers and, not least, in the Bible. Hammarskjöld's "mystery" is allied with what Paul says about the unsearchable judgments and inscrutable ways of God (Rom. 11:33) and about our "knowledge" as "partial"—"now we see in a mirror, dimly" (1 Cor. 13:12).

Let us conclude this part of our analysis with some remarks about mysticism and the use of the Bible in *Markings*. When mystics—rightly or wrongly so described—have made use of the Bible, they have usually turned chiefly to the writings of John and Paul. It would be an error to consider those writings "mystical," but there is much there that mystics can point to in support of their views. The fact is, however, that when Hammarskjöld turns to the Bible he almost never refers to utterances of this kind. He could easily have found biblical expressions complementary to his own more "mystical" writings. When he says, "Not I, but God in me," we cannot but remember Paul: "It is no longer I who live, but Christ who lives in me" (Gal. 2:20). When we hear Hammarskjöld's definition of faith, quoted from Saint John of the Cross: "Faith is God's union with the soul," we are reminded, for instance, of "God is love, and he who abides in love abides in God, and God abides in him" (1 John 4:16). But in *Markings* we find no such references. There are only one or two allusions to Paul. And there are merely a few references to the Gospel of John: one to the light shining in the darkness, another to the account of Jesus' washing the feet of the disciples—a picture of service most characteristic of Hammarskjöld.

It is significant that half of Hammarskjöld's quotations from the Bible are drawn from the Psalms and most of the other quotations are from the synoptic Gospels. He obviously used the Psalter as a devotional manual; his quotations from it begin in 1953, when his yes to God becomes apparent, and continue until the end of *Markings*—the end of his life. It was no accident that he found here the definition of faith as being in God's hands. The Psalms offer, he found, simple and clear statements and prayers describing what life in the hands of God means. The final quotation in *Markings,* dated August 1961, is Psalm 78:35: "And they remembered that God was their strength—" (p. 178).

There is no particular "mysticism" in the picture of life in the hands of God offered by the Psalms. But what about the references to the synoptic Gospels? Here Hammarskjöld's meditations are concentrated on the picture of Jesus—chiefly, the picture of Jesus on his way to the cross. With one exception these references offer no ground for "mystical" interpretation. The exception is the passage from the Good Friday 1956[4] marking in which Hammarskjöld writes of Jesus as dying "in someone who has followed the trail marks of the inner road to the end" (p. 111). If there is "mysticism" here, it is a Jesus-mysticism or Christ-mysticism. This in itself would be unique for *Markings,* since all other "mystical" passages refer to the Godhead himself and to union with him.

This Good Friday 1956 statement clearly describes an intimate relation to Jesus. It is not sophistry, however, to claim that the words about Jesus' dying in his followers have not a mystical but a symbolic character. The main perspective here—as at many other points—is, in *imitatio* to follow Jesus on the way of sacrifice. It would accordingly be wrong to find in this statement a "Christ-mysticism." If we are to see mysticism in *Markings,* it must be a God-mysticism. Such might be allowed—

[4] See pp. 48–49 above.

but only if it is remembered that Hammarskjöld could describe the same thing, the same relationship to God, without using the language of the medieval mystics: "God's union with the soul" is, from man's point of view, "to be in the hands of God."

Some Comparisons: Luther, Kierkegaard, and Bonhoeffer

It is appropriate—as we approach the end of our study—to draw comparisons between the views of Dag Hammarskjöld and those of certain other key figures in the history of religious thought. This can aid us in our quest for a proper understanding of *Markings* and its author. I propose, for this exercise in comparison, Martin Luther, Søren Kierkegaard, and Dietrich Bonhoeffer. None is quoted in *Markings*, but, as we shall demonstrate, comparisons remain relevant.

Luther is a ready and proper figure to study. Hammarskjöld's background was the "Lutheran" tradition of the Church of Sweden. That tradition, in his time, took many various shapes, and our purpose is not to sketch those different positions. It is worth observing, however, that during Hammarskjöld's life Sweden was the scene of an energetic investigation of Luther himself. A clear trend in this characteristically Swedish research was to emphasize the difference between Luther himself and later scholastic theology, the so-called Lutheran Orthodoxy. Luther was, to employ a barbarism, dedogmatized and approached without confessional bias as one of the truly pivotal teachers in Christian history as a whole.[5]

Hammarskjöld was not a professional theologian and, certainly, it would be meaningless to examine him from the outlook of a "Lutheran" theology, old or new. It is meaningful, however, to compare him with Luther himself. There is, in point of fact, no lack of affinity between the two, affinity which has not been sufficiently observed in the literature about Hammarskjöld. In a Swedish treatise on the "Christ-meditations" in *Markings*, Professor Hjalmar Sundén declares that the mysticism in *Markings* reveals a model of religious perception that is "un-Lutheran."[6]

[5] Cf. Edgar M. Carlson, *The Reinterpretation of Luther* (Philadelphia: Fortress, 1948).
[6] Hjalmar Sundén, *Kristusmeditationer i Dag Hammarskjölds Vägmärken* (Stockholm: Verbum, 1966), p. 73.

When discussing Hammarskjöld's relation to Luther and Lutheranism, Van Dusen makes the following statement: "In all of this, there is not the dimmest echo of the 'justification by faith' which was the very heart of Martin Luther's proclamation, and of the theology of the Churches which bear his name."[7] It is, to be sure, correct that the formula so intimately associated with Luther is not mentioned in *Markings*. That fact, however, proves nothing, since Luther was perfectly capable of stating his message without recourse to his familiar terms—as he did, for example, in the *Small Catechism*. It is not advisable, when interpreting Luther, to look only for fixed formulas. In spite of the attention Van Dusen pays to the relations between Archbishop Nathan Söderblom and the Hammarskjöld family, including Dag, he nevertheless seems to think that the "Lutheranism" Hammarskjöld knew in Sweden was only a stereotyped tradition, bound to formulas that had been shaped perhaps in the seventeenth century. That, however, was not the case.

I have not the slightest intention of modeling Hammarskjöld according to Luther or of presenting him as a "Lutheran." That, certainly, would be wrong: Hammarskjöld did not use Luther's categories, and there is no reason to force them upon him. My purpose is simply to register what, in fact, *Markings* does show concerning possible resemblances between the two figures.

We should remember first that for Luther, as for Hammarskjöld, the medieval mystics—notably two: Johannes Tauler and the *Theologia Germanica*—were of considerable importance. As is well known, there are, in Luther's writings, several statements which possess a marked mystical color. To quote two of these: "The Holy Spirit . . . makes man one mind and one spirit with God; thus his mind wills and asks, seeks and loves what God wills."[8] Another statement runs: "Love is the only, eternal, and unexpressible good and most high treasure which you call God himself, from whom everything flows and has its essence and, thus, subsists in and through the same love. Further, everyone who remains in this love remains in God, and God in him, and so he

---

[7] Henry Pitney Van Dusen, *Dag Hammarskjöld: The Statesman and His Faith* (New York: Harper, 1967), p. 179.
[8] From a sermon by Luther on Matt. 25:1–13 (Erlanger Ausgabe, 1st ed., vol. 15, pp. 24–25).

and God become one cake."⁹ Thus Luther in characteristically excessive language speaks of "God's union with the soul." Now this ought not to lead us to conclude that Luther's relation to mysticism was the same as Hammarskjöld's. Nevertheless, any interpretation of Luther is defective if it fails to consider that for Luther also faith was a communion with God in heart and mind that could be described in terms of mystic color.

However, there are other, more important, points of contact between our two figures. Three such points present themselves: the view of sin; "the freedom of a Christian"; and the understanding of vocation.

When Luther speaks of sin, one of his most characteristic and expressive descriptions of the meaning of sin is the Latin formula *incurvatus in se:* sin is, to be curved in upon oneself. Hammarskjöld seldom —in fact, I think, only once—uses the word *sin.* That does not, however, indicate that the reality is unknown to him. On the contrary: in *Markings* there is hardly a theme so constant and omnipresent as that of *incurvatus in se* or, in other words, self-centeredness. There is nothing condemned more severely by Hammarskjöld, nothing disclosed, prosecuted, and combatted more ruthlessly than self-centeredness. Further, his self-criticism does not cease with the experience of "God's union with the soul." On the contrary, "the religious reality forces 'the Night Side' out into light." This corresponds to what Luther says in, for example, his very characteristic declaration: *imo quo quisque magis pius est, hoc plus sentit illam pugnam.*¹⁰ These words can bear the following interpretation: the nearer you are to God in faith the more you will discover what it means to be curved into yourself, and, then, the more you will also fight against sin. Certainly, Hammarskjöld would agree; the dramatic perspective of Luther's declaration would be quite familiar to him.

Furthermore, there is a very obvious affinity between Hammarskjöld's position and Luther's famous treatise *The Freedom of a Christian,* in which he unfolds the thesis that a Christian "is a perfectly free lord

---

[9] From a sermon by Luther on 1 John 4:16 (Erlanger Ausgabe, 1st ed., vol. 19, p. 365).
[10] From Luther's commentary on Galatians of 1535 (Erlanger Ausgabe, lateinischer Teil [E Gal], vol. 3, p. 23).

of all, subject to none," and at the same time "a perfectly dutiful servant of all men, subject to all."[11] Both of these aspects are focal to *Markings,* where freedom is inseparably united with unreserved service. As soon as Hammarskjöld's *yes to God* appears in *Markings* it is immediately followed by passages which emphasize the freedom that is included in this relation to God: "He who has placed himself in God's hand stands free vis-à-vis men" (p. 88). "To be free, to be able to stand up and leave *everything* behind—without looking back. To say *Yes—*" (p. 88). "When his attention is directed beyond and above, how strong he is, with the strength of God who is within him because he is in God. Strong and free, because his self no longer exists" (p. 96).

This freedom, moreover, is to be realized in unreserved service to men. Freedom "is a freedom in the midst of action," and the action required is service, an action "for the sake of others." In a characteristic entry Hammarskjöld says: "To step out of all this, and stand naked on the precipice of dawn—accepted, invulnerable, free: in the Light, with the Light, of the Light. *Whole,* real in the Whole. Out of myself as a stumbling block, into myself as fulfillment" (p. 130*). Fulfillment means to realize oneself in and through service. "Out of myself" reminds us of some remarkable words of Luther's: in faith God *rapit nos a nobis*—he snatches us out of ourselves. Karl Holl, one of the important interpreters of Luther in our century, has demonstrated, in studying the Reformer's own self-consciousness, that Luther saw the Christian life in terms of a paradoxically acute relationship between unselfishness and self-confidence.[12] In fact, that is very like Hammarskjöld's way of combining complete self-surrender with self-realization: "Except in faith, nobody is humble. . . . And, except in faith, nobody is proud. . . . To be, in faith, both humble and proud: that is, to *live,* to know that in God I am nothing, but that God is in me" (p. 88).

We turn finally to the view of vocation as it appears in Luther and in *Markings.* It ought first to be noted that in both cases we find a

[11] *Luther's Works,* vol. 31, *Career of the Reformer: I* (Philadelphia: Fortress, 1957), p. 344.
[12] Cf. Karl Holl, "Martin Luther on Luther," trans. H. C. Erik Midelfort, in *Interpreters of Luther,* ed. Jaroslav Pelikan (Philadelphia: Fortress, 1968), pp. 9–34.

strong consciousness of having received a special "call." There is no need to explain in detail Luther's conception of the call.[13] As regards Hammarskjöld, we have already examined what it meant to him to have been "dedicated": Hammarskjöld did not say that God appointed him to be the Secretary General of the United Nations, but he nevertheless received the charge entrusted to him, including all its responsibility, as a divine vocation.

The question of vocation ought rather to be seen from another point of view. We ought to take into consideration Luther's assertion that service to God can be performed in every charge, every vocation, without discrimination. The monastery had no prerogative over "worldly" charges that in one or another way offered service to men. The decisive question did not concern the character of the charge, but faithfulness in the service. According to a well-known utterance of Luther's, the servant girl cleaning a room with her broom performed an act pleasing to God.[14] This was a perspective cherished by Hammarskjöld: "How poor is the courage which knows its 'why,' compared to the quiet heroism an unreflective mind can display in the most inglorious and degrading trials" (p. 115). A vocation can be fulfilled in a way that is not at all ostentatious; it can be fully performed more or less in secret, in an anonymous manner.

Luther's view showed a new openness towards the world, and, no doubt, this openness is similar to an essential element in Hammarskjöld's own view of vocation. It can, indeed, be described as prerequisite to the conception of the life of action unfolded in *Markings*. In his work on behalf of world peace, Hammarskjöld was daily confronted with all the problems and needs of the world. This gave a new accent to his understanding of vocation as service to men: the obligation to help in a world in need is chiefly an obligation not of charity but of righteousness. This insight returns again and again in Hammarskjöld's speeches —even as the word *righteousness* appears again and again in *Markings*. But the service of men is at the same time a service of God, flowing out of and receiving inspiration and strength from union with God—

---

[13] Cf. Gustaf Wingren, *Luther on Vocation*, trans. Carl C. Rasmussen (Philadelphia: Fortress, 1957).

[14] This same point is made in Roland H. Bainton, *Here I Stand: A Life of Martin Luther* (Nashville: Abingdon, 1950), p. 234.

thus a service performed in self-surrender and self-sacrifice. In this sense and with these double references Hammarskjöld could say that, in our era, the way to sanctification passes through action. These words could hardly have been used in the same way by Luther; nevertheless they stand closer to Luther himself than to much later "Lutheranism."

Before we leave Luther, it is fitting to comment on the role forgiveness plays in *Markings*. For Luther the forgiveness of sin is the principal word above all others: "Where there is forgiveness of sins, there are also life and salvation."[15] In *Markings* God's forgiveness is mentioned first in 1956. But "forgiveness" is implied in the earlier descriptions of union with God and of life in his hand—clearly implied, for example, in Hammarskjöld's affirmation of the new freedom realized in this relationship—a relationship of faith—to God. We have observed that forgiveness was more and more emphasized in Hammarskjöld's later years and also that his view of forgiveness and its conditions was then modified to a certain degree. In *Markings*, however, we do not meet the same radicalism concerning the forgiving divine love, the *agape* of God, as we do in Luther and the New Testament. Here we are not considering Hammarskjöld's oft-repeated affirmation that God's forgiveness must be combined with our forgiveness of others. At Easter 1960 he said, "The price you must pay for your own liberation through another's sacrifice is that you in turn must be willing to liberate in the same way, irrespective of the consequences to yourself" (p. 163); he would be completely misunderstood if he were interpreted as offering a prerequisite for God's forgiveness. His intention is simply to emphasize that God's forgiveness must result in an unrestricted willingness to forgive others—a repeated assertion of the Gospels.

Nevertheless, it is obvious that Hammarskjöld found it difficult to discover or acknowledge the whole of the radicalism of the New Testament and Luther. In any discussion of Luther we must pay attention to the dominant role that "the word" plays in his writings: to acknowledge the forgiveness of God means to cling to and abide by the word of God as it appears in the sayings and actions of Jesus, and throughout the biblical testimony to Christ. We find no such reference to the word of God in *Markings*. But certainly we find there a counterpart to Luther's view: the dominant role that the sacrifice of Jesus played

[15] Martin Luther, *The Small Catechism*, part 6.

for Hammarskjöld as early as the time of his crisis and subsequently through *Markings* can, no doubt, be considered a concentrated "word of God." In this he heard a summons to *imitatio,* a summons to follow Jesus on the way of sacrifice. His view of the meaning of sacrifice, as we know, deepened by degrees; sacrifice came to be seen as the divine creative power.

At Easter 1960 the result of this development appears: divine forgiveness "entails a sacrifice." *Imitatio* always dominates in *Markings,* but that does not necessarily imply a reticence in respect to the radical *agape.* In the three synoptic Gospels there is a strong accent on *imitatio* and, at the same time, an explanation of radical, divine *agape* which operates, not in the conditional mood, but fully, without restriction. At the point of *imitatio,* Hammarskjöld is unquestionably much more in harmony with the Gospels than is the Lutheran tradition, which has often suppressed and neglected this aspect of the Christian life. Hammarskjöld's reticence concerning radical *agape* is obviously connected with his radical self-criticism. Certainly, without self-criticism the radical *agape* is only a caricature—but without radical *agape* the burden of self-criticism is infinitely harder to bear. Even if there is in *Markings* an obvious reticence concerning the radicalism of God's *agape,* that has not hindered Hammarskjöld from accepting the divine forgiveness as a liberating gift. Moreover, even those who have discovered the Gospels' message of radical *agape* may have great difficulty in applying this discovery to themselves.

With these remarks, we leave Luther. Much more could be said about the affinity between Hammarskjöld and him—about the "hidden" God, for instance. And much more could also be said about the differences between them. However, these brief remarks may have proven a sufficient introduction to a fascinating set of parallels. The fact that Hammarskjöld himself never seems to have reflected on his relations to Luther makes the study more interesting.

In Chapter One of the present study mention was made of how the Danish diplomat Eyvind Bartels has contrasted Hammarskjöld and Søren Kierkegaard. Bartels sees a certain spiritual resemblance between the two; but he claims that, in contrast to Hammarskjöld, Kierkegaard possessed a deep and genuine Christian faith. Bartels ends his comparison of the two men with the perplexing statement that Kierkegaard had "a human heart such as, in my opinion, we seek in vain in Hammarskjöld's writings."[16] I consider this strange declaration to be a challenge to compare the positions of these men more precisely. We shall, of course, disregard the cardiac specialist's statement about the difference between their "hearts."

What about their affinity? At one point in our examination of Hammarskjöld's faith, we said that it had an "existential" character. In our time Kierkegaard has often been designated a father of existentialist philosophy and theology. There is no need to point out that Hammarskjöld is far removed from this category of thinkers. Nevertheless, his view of faith as "existential" and as involving the whole being of man has, no doubt, some resemblance to Kierkegaard's position, and Hammarskjöld could very well have given assent to the Dane's judgment that faith entails a transformation of the entire quality of one's being. We ought not, however, to draw any far-reaching conclusions from this similarity. Furthermore, the resemblance might seem considerable in light of the fact that both Kierkegaard and Hammarskjöld make extensive use of at least one common word, *imitatio,* and that both of them use that word to explain faith's proper relation to life. It quickly becomes apparent, however, that they actually possessed only the word in common: their interpretations reveal a wide distance between them.

Let us look first at Kierkegaard's interpretation of *imitatio* and sacrifice. As he emphasizes that the entire Christian life must consist in following Christ, *imitatio* comes to mean following the pattern of the suffering and persecuted Christ. It can be described by Kierkegaard as "sheer suffering, groaning, and lamentation, heightened by a background of judgment in which every word must be accounted for . . . a terrible series of suffering, *Angst,* and trembling."[17] No doctrine is for Kierkegaard more focal than the doctrine of suffering. A life stamped by suffering is at the same time a life of martyrdom, and the highest token

---
[16] See p. 3 above.
[17] Soren Kierkegaard, *The Last Years: Journals 1853–1855,* ed. and trans. Ronald Gregor Smith (New York: Harper, 1965), pp. 320 ff. For an interesting essay on related problems, cf. "Soren Kierkegaard on Luther," by Ernest B. Koenker, in *Interpreters of Luther* (see n. 12 above), pp. 231–52.

of martyrdom is death. It is typical that one of Kierkegaard's many objections to Luther was that he did not crown his work with the death of a martyr and thus show himself to be a true reformer.

The radical demand of the law was thus, for Kierkegaard, to train for eternity on the way of suffering. Suffering, however, also implies blessedness—the more suffering, the more blessedness. Accordingly, Kirkegaard also speaks of suffering as gospel, "the gospel of our sufferings." Law and gospel consequently flow together into one stream. Notable in this picture of life is the consistent assertion that suffering comes from God, an assertion which lays bare one of the most crucial elements in Kirkegaard's thought: the decisive contrast between eternity and time, between God's infinite majesty and man's life in a finite world. It is just this contrast that produces suffering and that bit by bit sharpens and intensifies the radical demand to suffer as preparation for eternity. The result of these ideas is that the proper relation to the world becomes a very negative one that culminates in a renunciation of the world, in infinite resignation, even in hostility towards the world. Such a view obviously leads to an extreme individualism: the Christian is, according to Kierkegaard, "alone," a solitary individual before the transcendent majesty.

In light of Kierkegaard's interpretation of what the imitation of Christ means, it is not difficult to discover the wide distance between Hammarskjöld and him. *Imitatio Christi* was most important to Hammarskjöld too, but for him it did not mean an emulation of the pattern of Jesus' life of suffering. Where Kierkegaard dwells on suffering, Hammarskjöld speaks of sacrifice, and sacrifice means primarily self-surrender and self-sacrifice—*for the sake of others*. It is true that Hammarskjöld, like Kierkegaard, had a good deal to say about death, and it might seem that his contemplations of death reveal a basic kinship between the two. Yet the difference can easily be made clear. Hammarskjöld does not speak of death as crowning martyrdom; he rather speaks of death as a fulfillment. This view is concentrated in a passage in *Markings* where, after having said that death ought not to be sought, he continues: "But seek the *road* [italics mine] which makes death a fulfillment" (p. 136). It can correctly be stated that Hammarskjöld here has in mind the road where "death" from the dominion of self-centeredness is continuous, and where life thus becomes a sacrifice of self for the sake of others. In this perspective death as the end of earthly life is a "fulfillment."

The great distance between Kierkegaard and Hammarskjöld is made crystal clear in their different views of suffering. Hammarskjöld does not think that suffering comes from God, nor that it follows from a contrast between the infinite and the finite. "That piece of blasphemous anthropomorphism: the belief that, in order to educate us, God wishes us to suffer" (p. 138*). Suffering is an evil and as such does not come from God. The decisive question regarding suffering is—as the entire passage from *Markings* which we have just quoted shows—how the burden of suffering is endured: whether in obedience to the will of God or not.

Beyond all of this, however, the deepest chasm between Hammarskjöld and Kierkegaard is found at the point of their different relations to "the world." For Kierkegaard the radical demand involves renunciation of the world, even hostility to it. The "action" thus called for is first and foremost to train for eternity with an infinite resignation towards all that belongs to life in time, towards all that is "finite." For Hammarskjöld, on the other hand, union with God must be realized in the world, through the service of men—and this service cannot be realized without self-sacrifice. Here are two strikingly different views of the "radical demand."

For Hammarskjöld the decisive contrast is not—as for Kierkegaard—between the infinite and the finite; it is rather betwen good and evil. This is why Hammarskjöld's position requires an openness towards the world which is to be manifested in the service of men. It is at this point that Hammarskjöld's position diverges greatly from Kierkegaard's, for Kierkegaard the radical demand involves, not service to others in this finite world, but training for eternity on the way of suffering and self-chosen martyrdom. At the point of this particular contrast, it is difficult to imagine a view of Christianity more inhuman and, in its consequences, more cruel than Kierkegaard's. This conclusion is underscored by Knud Løgstrup, the prominent Danish Kierkegaard scholar, in his essay, "Encounter with Kierkegaard": "According to Kierkegaard's intepretation of Christianity, God does not act as Lord for the sake of the life that he has created. His demand does not serve human life, and it does not receive its content from the life God has created. In Kierkegaard's view of Christianity, the demand on man is a demand for the sake of salvation. That explains why Kierkegaard rapidly screws up the demand from being radical to being cruel. No created life is able to give content to the demand—there is only a life to be annihilated by the demand and, through the annihilation, to pay ·for salvation. Salvation, in itself law, emancipates the law from created life. Law and creation have nothing to do with each other. When salvation is eternal bliss, and when it appears as law, this law cannot be severe enough. It can only become a claim to the annihilation of human life."[18]

Hammarskjöld's openness towards the world is indissolubly connected with his faith in God. Faith as union with God or as being in God's hand must be realized in action, and the action must necessarily be service to men. He knows that his efforts to realize this service are inadequate—the last prayer in Markings is a prayer for forgiveness—but at the same time he knows that there is no other way. The demand of God—the other side of his gift—is imperative and inevitable.

Why compare Hammarskjöld with Bonhoeffer? There are several justifications, but chiefly two: Bonhoeffer and Hammarskjöld were contemporaries—in fact, Bonhoeffer was born half a year after Hammarskjöld—and there are, I think, obvious positive relationships between the view of Christianity found in Bonhoeffer's *Letters and Papers from Prison* and that in *Markings*. We can anticipate our conclusion: that which separates Hammarskjöld from Kierkegard is at the same time that which constitutes his affinity to Bonhoeffer.

Few books, in recent times, have had a greater influence than Bonhoeffer's *Widerstand und Ergebung,* known in the English-speaking world as *Letters and Papers from Prison*.[19] This book is—like *Markings*

---

[18] Knud E. Logstrup, "Opgor med Kierkegaard," in *Festskrift til N. H. Soe* (Copenhagen: G. E. C. Gad, 1965), p. 108.

[19] Dietrich Bonhoeffer, *Letters and Papers from Prison,* ed. Eberhard Bethge, trans. Reginald H. Fuller et al., 3d ed., rev. and enl. (New York: Macmillan, 1967).

—posthumous. Bonhoeffer was executed by the Nazis in April 1945, in the last month of Hitler's government of terror. The book, first published in 1951, contains letters and some aphoristic sketches—it is not a coherent interpretation of Christianity. However, in spite of its fragmentary character it has become an inspiration the marks of which can be found among Christians everywhere. In fact, this book has been enormously influential, not only by virtue of its own views, but also because of the way it has been seriously misunderstood as a result of the strange terminology Bonhoeffer sometimes uses.

In prison Bonhoeffer gave thorough consideration to the situation of faith "in our era"—to use Hammarskjöld's words. This consideration was characterized by a radical openness towards "the world." Bonhoeffer wrote in a situation where his own death was always imminent; yet he was intensely occupied with the problem of Christianity in relation to the world. He was surrounded by the most horrible caricatures of human maturity; and yet he wrote about the world come of age.

One of the most striking features of the letters is Bonhoeffer's energetic fight *against* religious individualism and exclusiveness and *for* a "wordly," nonreligious interpretation of Christianity. It is no wonder that such terminology is easily misunderstood. The word *religion* has here ceased to be positive; it has become a negative notion. Misunderstandings will be inevitable if one is not aware of the fact that "religion" is for Bonhoeffer an egocentric and isolating piety. Bonhoeffer has been interpreted as if he were advocating a pure secularity, but certainly he is not. On the contrary, his dominating concern is how Christ can be the Lord of the nonreligious.

Bonhoeffer fights on two fronts.[20] Against a false otherworldliness represented by a self-centered piety which tries to keep itself isolated from the world, he emphasizes *die Diesseitigkeit,* the "this-worldliness" of Christianity—the life of the Christian who lives and acts in the midst of the needs of the world. God is then seen not only as meeting men at the frontiers of life, but as encountering them in the midst of life. He does not meet men only in their weakness; he also meets

[20] Cf. Benkt-Erik Benktson, *Christus und die Religion: Der Religionsbegriff bei Barth, Bonhoeffer, und Tillich* (Stuttgart: Calwer, 1967), pp. 43, 74.

them in their strength. In the midst of life, however, God meets men as *jenseitig*, as the One who is "otherwise" or, to use Hammarskjöld's expression, as "the Other." Bonhoeffer thus also fights against a *false* "this-worldliness." The "this-worldliness" he advocates is not commonplace or platitudinous. He does not strive for a world or a life without God—"God-is-dead theology" has nothing to obtain from Bonhoeffer. To be sure, there is in Bonhoeffer's view a "God" who is dead, but it is not the God of the Bible. It is the "God" who is viewed as "prolonged world" or as "metaphysical" essence, the "God" who acts as a moralistic guardian of men who are incapable of managing their own affairs. And at this point we are reminded of the sense in which Hammarskjöld writes of an "independence" from God insofar as man has a responsibility of his own for all of his actions.[21]

In Hammarskjöld we find none of the polemics of the theologian, still less the strange interpretation of the world *religion*. But we do find the same openness towards the world manifest both in Hammarskjöld's remarkable statement about action's being, in our era, the road to sanctification and in his consistent combination of union with God and action in the service of men. It ought to be observed that Bonhoeffer in one of his letters speaks of sanctification as one of the much-used words which now need a "worldly" interpretation.[22] He would have been pleased at the view offered by Hammarskjöld.

The degree of affinity between Hammarskjöld and Bonhoeffer will be most apparent when we examine how the way of action is to be derived from "faith." Hammarskjöld writes chiefly about relationship to God, Bonhoeffer chiefly about relationship to Christ. This is a difference in emphasis but not in actual content. In one of his last letters, dated August 21, 1944, Bonhoeffer says that "if we are to learn what God promises, and what he fulfils, we must persevere in quiet meditation on the life, sayings, deeds, sufferings, and death of Jesus. It is certain that we may always live close to God and in the light of his presence, and that such living is an entirely new life for us: that nothing is then impossible for us, because all things are possible with God."[23] A parallel

---

[21] See pp. 96–98 above.
[22] Bonhoeffer, *Letters and Papers*, p. 145.
[23] Ibid., p. 206.

statement in *Markings* asserts that union with God means "certainty of God's omnipotence *through* the soul: with God all things are possible, *because* faith can move mountains" (p. 115).

Hammarskjöld put his decisive question concerning Jesus and his sacrifice in this fashion: Only for the sake of others—or . . .? "For the sake of others" thus became a watchword for the rest of his life. Bonhoeffer, in notes written in August of 1944, writes, "Who is God? Not in the first place an abstract belief in God, in his omnipotence etc. That is not a genuine experience of God, but a partial extension of the world. Encounter with Jesus Christ. The experience that a transformation of all human life is given in the fact that 'Jesus is there only for others.' His 'being there for others' is the experience of transcendence. It is only this 'being there for others,' maintained till death, that is the ground of his omnipotence, omniscience, and omnipresence. . . . Our relation to God is a new life in 'existence for others,' through participation in the being of Jesus."[24]

Participation in the life of Jesus meant for Bonhoeffer, as for Hammarskjöld, *imitatio,* a word which is of great importance for both. Bonhoeffer in his early days wrote about *Nachfolge (Imitatio)*,[25] and in the letters from prison he indicated that he would like once more to take up this subject.[26] The imitation of Jesus will be realized in actions of self-sacrifice. At the same time, imitation means to take seriously "not our own sufferings, but those of God in the world—watching with Christ in Gethsemane."[27] This calls to mind Hammarskjöld's Good Friday meditation.[28] "Man," Bonhoeffer says, "is summoned to share in God's sufferings at the hands of a godless world."[29] This, however, does not mean that suffering is to be the principle of life—that was, according to Bonhoeffer, the fault of "existentialist philosophy" (may we say, Kierkegaard?) which led to a "secularized methodism."[30]

---

[24] Ibid., p. 202.
[25] This work of Bonhoeffer's has been published in English under the title *The Cost of Discipleship* (trans. Reginald H. Fuller, 2d ed., unabr. and rev. [New York: Macmillan, 1959]).
[26] Bonhoeffer, *Letters and Papers,* p. 86.
[27] Ibid., p. 193.
[28] See pp. 48–49 above.
[29] Ibid., p. 190.
[30] Ibid., p. 169.

According to Bonhoeffer, to be a Christian does not mean to be confined to any fixed "religious" attitude: "To be a Christian does not mean to be religious in a particular way . . . but to be a man—not a type of man, but the man that Christ creates in us."[31] The intention of such a statement is very similar to a basic emphasis in *Markings:* union with God creates the integrity of man, "the wonder: that *I* exist" (p. 102), and "a humble and spontaneous response to Life" (p. 147). In Bonhoeffer's terminology, life in the presence of God means a true "coming of age," and, then, "the world's coming of age" will be "better understood than it understands itself."[32] From life with such a center "we ought to find and love God in what he actually gives us"[33]—love towards God is "a kind of *cantus firmus* to which the other melodies of life provide the counterpoint."[34] In *Markings* we read that union with God means "to love life and men as God loves them" (p. 112), it means "an unbroken living contact with all things" (p. 147).

The affinity between Hammarskjöld and Bonhoeffer which we have described is the more interesting inasmuch as their views developed independently of each other—yet, most significantly, both lived and acted "in our era."

The Profile of Hammarskjöld's Faith

I have borrowed the word *profile* from Hammarskjöld's letter to Leif Belfrage, published at the beginning of *Markings*. Hammarskjöld writes, "These entries provide the only true 'profile' that can be drawn" (p. 7). Regarding this statement, the translator W. H. Auden says in his Foreword: "Even if the book were as extensive and detailed a 'confession' as those of Boswell or Rousseau or Gide, this statement would still be false. No man can draw his own 'profile' correctly. . . . The truth is that our friends—and our enemies—always know us better than we know ourselves."[35] Auden's remark is true enough; nevertheless I suspect that he

---

[31] Ibid., p. 190.
[32] Ibid., p. 172.
[33] Ibid., p. 94.
[34] Ibid., p. 150.
[35] W. H. Auden, Foreword to *Markings,* by Dag Hammarskjöld, trans. Leif Sjöberg and W. H. Auden (London: Faber and Faber, 1964), p. 11.

gives to Hammarskjöld's statement a wider meaning than it originally had. It is not very likely that a man as hypercritical as Hammarskjöld would have been unaware of the limitations inherent in autobiography. It seems to me that Hammarskjöld meant, in his letter, to say two simple things: first, the diary *is* an open disclosure of "my negotiations with myself—and with God"; and, second, every attempt at biography that does not take into consideration what this diary discloses will inevitably draw a wrong "profile."

The aim of our present study has not been to write a biographical or psychological study of Hammarskjöld's life. Its purpose has been simply to analyze the faith which appears in *Markings*. Our present question thus becomes: Has the *faith* of which *Markings* renders account any "profile" of its own?

Before we go on, let us recall to mind something Hammarskjöld says in his important statement of 1953—something that has been interpreted in different ways. Hammarskjöld says there that he has been "led in a circle": "I now recognize and endorse, unreservedly, those very beliefs which were once handed down to me."[36]

Hjalmar Sundén, the Swedish interpreter of Hammarskjöld's "Christ-meditations" has insisted that on the whole the passages in *Markings* which deal with Christ are "undogmatic" and even "heretical." The same critic, however, notes a swing to "orthodoxy" at those points when Hammarskjöld considers the great Christian festivals; he cites especially the passages from Easter and Christmas 1960. According to this view, Hammarskjöld's "circle" was one from "orthodoxy" via "heterodoxy" back to "orthodoxy."[37] Such an interpretation is not only couched in terms which would have been quite meaningless to Hammarskjöld, but it is also—as we have already established—thoroughly false. Even though a large number of crucial passages in *Markings* were written on or around great Christian festivals, no case can be made for claiming that Hammarskjöld had any special "festival-day faith."

Far more interesting is Henry Pitney Van Dusen's interpretation of Hammarskjöld's words about the "circle." He suggests that this self-interpretation was not quite accurate: "If a spatial figure were to be used,

[36] Hammarskjöld, "Old Creeds," p. 23.
[37] Sundén, *Kristusmeditationer*, pp. 72–85.

· 139 ·

it would more properly be a spiral rather than a circle. His conviction returned to the same basic certitudes, but at a higher level."[38] This higher level Van Dusen describes as "a far more sophisticated and far richer, a more subtle and more comprehensively classical Christian experience and certitude."[39] Certainly, no basic objection can be raised against this description; we must, however, put one crucial question to Van Dusen. According to him, there is in Hammarskjöld's final faith "hardly a discoverable trace . . . of the rather rigid scholastic Swedish Lutheranism in which he had been reared and in which he must have been instructed before Confirmation into membership in the Church of Sweden."[40]

At this point I must call on personal knowledge. The pastor who provided Dag Hammarskjöld's catechetical instruction was with me a member of the clergy in the Diocese of Strängnäs, where I was for twenty years bishop. From that clergyman the young Hammarskjöld never received instruction in any "rigid scholastic Lutheranism." Nor did Hammarskjöld encounter such scholasticism during his academic years at Uppsala, where he was in close contact with Archbishop Nathan Söderblom. If his "foundation" had been scholastic Lutheranism, then his final faith would best be characterized in terms of contrast rather than with the image of a spiral. It is indeed true that the faith disclosed in *Markings* is not typically "Lutheran," but it is not true that no traces of a "Lutheran" heritage are discoverable in the book. How, then, are Hammarskjöld's words about the circle to be interpreted? His reference is to "the very beliefs that were once handed down to me," and obviously what he has in mind is not the ethical views of his father and mother. These views he never called into question. In referring to "beliefs" he no doubt has those of the Christian faith in mind. This should not be viewed narrowly in terms of any special type of faith, still less in terms of some series of fixed doctrines. What he wanted to say was, I think, quite simply that he had been led back to Christian faith and that—after years of skepticism and struggle—he now could confess that faith "in the light of experience and honest thinking." Thus the word *circle* possesses a high degree of accuracy, although its use does not obviate the

[38] Van Dusen, *Dag Hammarskjöld*, p. 177.
[39] Ibid., p. 50.
[40] Ibid., p. 49.

THE PROFILE OF HAMMARSKJÖLD'S FAITH

correctness of the figure of the "spiral." Hammarskjöld's mature interpretation of the Christian faith is not identical to what he met in his youth; it has a profile of its own.

Before we sketch this profile it might be appropriate to discuss Hammarskjöld's relation to the church. It has been said that "the Church holds no place whatever in Hammarskjöld's recognition."[41] Such an absolute statement cannot be substantiated. *Church* is a word of different meanings, and Hammarskjöld's relation to the church can also be considered from different points of view. There can be no doubt that the church as "the communion of saints" did mean much to him. We remember his important statement of 1952, indicative of progress towards his yes: "This vision of a magnetic field in the soul, created in a timeless present by unknown multitudes, living in holy obedience, whose words and actions are a timeless prayer. —'The Communion of Saints'—and—within it—an eternal life" (p. 84). Another statement, made later, in a time of more pronounced faith, emphasizes strongly the deep importance of the communion of saints for existence as a whole: "How would the moral sense of Reason—and of Society—have evolved without the martyrs of the faith? Indeed, how could this moral sense have escaped withering away, had it not constantly been watered by the feeder-stream of power that issues from those who have lost their selves in God? The rope over the abyss is held taut by those who, faithful to a faith which is the perpetual ultimate sacrifice, give it anchorage in Heaven." Characteristically Hammarskjöld then ends by accentuating the claim and the risk of being involved in such a life: "Those who, in 'God's union with the soul,' have been judged to be the salt of the earth—woe betide them, if the salt should lose its savor" (p. 96 *).

There is yet another important indication of Hammarskjöld's contact with the church's way of living, namely, the fact that much in *Markings* is written on or around the great Christian festivals. Surely no one who seemed so continually aware of the Church Year should be viewed without reference to the church as such.

The assumption that Hammarskjöld seldom attended church services has frequently been made and discussed. There may be rather good reason for Auden's view that any public commitment to a particular Chris-

[41] Ibid., p. 205.

tian body during his tenure as Secretary General of the United Nations would have labeled him as too "Western." Bo Beskow has another explanation: "Dag was not a church-going person. . . . We were both afraid of bad sermons, having been spoilt by growing up with great preachers like Nathan Söderblom, who was a close friend of both our families, and my father, who was constantly read in Dag's family."[42] However, the statement that Hammarskjöld was not a churchgoing person must be modified to say more accurately that he was not a regular attendant at services of worship. His brother, Governor Bo Hammarskjöld, has written to me about Dag's church attendance in the following way: "Dag reported to me that in New York he was accustomed to slip into services of worship (in churches of varying denomination) whenever he had a free Sunday hour."

Bo Beskow's statement, however, is all the more interesting because of its indication that the books of Nathanael Beskow were frequently read in the Hammarskjöld household. The elder Beskow (1865–1953) was a remarkable lay preacher whose books of "sermonic essays" were widely used in Sweden. We must add that this reference to Nathanael Beskow only underlines the fact that at home Hammarskjöld was not nurtured on "rigid scholastic Lutheranism"; by no stretch of the imagination could Beskow ever be associated with that tradition.[43]

One additional comment concerning Hammarskjöld's attendance at formal worship is appropriate. The Meditation Room at the United Nations in New York was prepared under Hammarskjöld's personal direction, with Bo Beskow contributing extensively to its design and execution. It may well be that, subconsciously at least, the much-harried Secretary General was, in this room, providing for himself a compensatory and accessible place for worship.

We have seen that the church as the communion of saints had considerable meaning for Hammarskjöld. But what did he think about the churches as institutions? *Markings* gives us no help with this question. However, his view concerning the responsibility and the possibilities of

---
[42] Bo Beskow, *Dag Hammarskjöld: Strictly Personal* (Garden City, N. Y.: Doubleday, 1969), pp. 133–34.
[43] Cf. Yngve Brilioth, *A Brief History of Preaching*, trans. Karl E. Mattson (Philadelphia: Fortress, 1965), p. 214.

the churches is very clearly expressed in his address to the Second Assembly of the World Council of Churches held in Evanston, Illinois, in 1954.[44] The spiritual background of this address is to be found in some of the principal ideas of *Markings*—although the audience in Evanston, which knew nothing of *Markings,* could hardly have imagined how deeply the perspectives expressed in the address were anchored in Hammarskjöld's own views of faith and action. As would be expected, he underlined those purposes shared in common by the churches and the United Nations. He also underlined the fact that Christian faith must necessarily possess a universal perspective. In a characteristic way he referred at this point to the cross: "The Cross, although it is the unique fact on which the Christian Churches base their hope, should not separate those of Christian faith from others but should instead be that element in their lives which enables them to stretch out their hands to peoples of other creeds in the feeling of universal brotherhood." By thus pointing to the cross, he could refer to the Assembly's main theme, "Christ the Hope of the World," and at the same time indicate something quite in harmony with his own view of the sacrifice performed on the cross. There is a universal perspective in the words he wrote on Good Friday of 1956: "Jesus dies in someone who has followed the trail marks of the inner road to the end" (p. 111).

Hammarskjöld's address at Evanston reveals a most significant concern for the role of the churches in world affairs. After having said that "in speaking for justice, truth and trust in public affairs, the Churches may be a decisive force for good in international and national political life, without assuming a political role," he asks, "Can or should the Churches go any further?" He answers by stating, "In my view there is one thing they could do. They could help to explain how world affairs are run and what is the responsibility of every one of us." The meaning of such an "explanation" and "responsibility" he has unfolded in the preceding part of his address. It concerns "social and economic equality within the nations" and "equal rights and opportunities for all nations." This includes practical action, helping the underdeveloped countries "to

---

[44] Dag Hammarskjöld, "An Instrument of Faith," in *Servant of Peace* (see n. 1 above), pp. 56–61. Unless otherwise indicated, the quotations immediately following are from this speech.

achieve such economic progress as would give them their proper share in the wealth of the world" and to achieve the political stability necessary to independence. It includes also a response to the "need for inspiration, for the creation of a spirit among the leaders of the peoples which helps them to use the forces which they have to master, for peace and not for war, for evolution and not for revolution." The responsibility which Hammarskjöld thus asks the churches to share is one of worldwide perspective.

When he lays this charge of explanation upon the churches, Hammarskjöld also accentuates two elements characteristic of his own faith: "he who fears God will no longer fear men," and a biblical word of importance to himself: we should take no thought of the morrow—"for the morrow shall take thought for the things of itself. Sufficient unto the day is the evil thereof." Here is a call to hope and patience for long-term planning which is not a counsel of despair.

Hammarskjöld will thus not "politicize" the churches, but he certainly wants from them far more activity regarding, as he puts it, "the sickness of our world." In his youth he had been witness to the beginning of the Life and Work Movement among the churches (Stockholm, 1925). Were he living now, he would see more definite signs that his visions are perhaps moving towards reality. He demanded great things of the churches, and he had a high estimate of their possibilities. Yet I wonder if he did not view the churches very much in the same way as the United Nations: as institutions or organizations they were feeble creations of men's hands—but, from another point of view, they were marked by both human and superhuman goals.

We turn again to our final question: Has the faith explicated in *Markings* a "profile" of its own?

Markings, as a book, has an obviously aphoristic character. Much of it, especially that which dates from the time of Hammarskjöld's association with the United Nations, was probably written at the end of days of long and arduous labor. In light of the difficult circumstances under which the book was written, we would not be surprised if the diary were disparate and fragmentary. But it is not. On the contrary, one of the most remarkable features of *Markings* is its consistency and continuity.

The consistency appears immediately in the fact that such words as *duty, service, responsibility,* and *sacrifice* are regular words used with related meanings throughout the book. To be sure, *Markings* is an exposition of two radically different positions: (1) a skepticism that is transformed into (2) a very definite confession of faith, a clear *yes* to God. Nevertheless, two things about this transformation ought to be noted.

First, the yes that came into view at New Year's 1953 had been growing for a long time; glimpses had been in sight many times during years of hard struggle. The yes had been said secretly in a time not recognized even by Hammarskjöld himself. The yes had existed before it dawned on his consciousness. In 1954 Hammarskjöld wrote in a remarkable way about this hidden continuity: "Then I saw that the wall had never been there, that the 'unheard-of' is here and this, not something and somewhere else" (p. 90). This "wall" may be the same as "the frontier of the unheard-of"—a frontier first seen as a barrier which separated. But by 1954 Hammarskjöld had discovered that, in fact, the wall had never been there.

Second, the yes did not carry with it a consummation. It meant rather that the "growing" yes was of necessity a yes in constant growth and struggle. Yes to God meant, certainly, that something new had come; it meant union with God, living in the hands of God, receiving rest and strength from him—and thus it also meant new integrity for the "I," "the wonder that *I* am," integrity instead of chaos, freedom instead of the bondage of self-centeredness. But page after page in *Markings* shows that —through the last prayer of the final year—this faith was constantly in struggle, at battle. It was a faith at battle with the risks of returning chaos and ever threatening self-centeredness.

When asserting that *Markings* is truly consistent, however, I have in mind chiefly the view of faith developed in the diary. And here I must add the word *comprehensive.* To be sure, there are tensions in Hammarskjöld's view of faith. But tensions do not exclude consistency—in fact, no Christian faith exists apart from tension, since tension is one of the signs of faith's liveliness. *Markings* exhibits, from 1953 to 1961, a series of intimate interconnections in which one passage serves to interpret another. Exegesis—if that is not too academic a term—reveals a consistency which at first glance is far from apparent.

The consistency of the faith found in *Markings* gives to that faith a character of its own and, consequently, a profile of its own. This has been played down by W. H. Auden in his Foreword to the English edition of *Markings*. He finds Hammarskjöld always interesting when disclosing his personal experiences. But "when he is making general statements about the nature of the spiritual life or the 'noughting' of the self, one feels one has read it all before somewhere." Then Auden asserts: "He lacks the originality of insight into general problems displayed by such contemporaries as Simone Weil, for example, or Charles Williams."[45] In response to this judgment some comments ought to be made. First, if Christian faith has a character of its own, its every elaboration must contain at least some statements also found in other presentations. Further, if Hammarskjöld "lacks the originality of insight into general problems" that can be discovered in certain contemporaries, he nevertheless possesses a rare insight. His living combination of the contemplation of "union with God" with a life of worldly action stands unique among men who have given us their innermost "confessions."

Of course, Hammarskjöld never intended to construct a theological system, and *Markings* bears no resemblance to such an enterprise. His diary touched only on such questions as were vital to him personally. From the formal point of view of systematic thought his confessions can correctly be considered no more than a torso—which in itself, however, justifies no criticisms of *Markings*. After all, Hammarskjöld cannot reasonably be criticized for failing in what he never intended to do. Nevertheless, in *Markings* he has given not merely a series of disparate or atomistic aphorisms; he has rather provided, we maintain, a clear, consistent, and comprehensive view of what faith meant to him. This provision is for us the important thing. We have a surfeit of theological systems, but we have no books of confession like Hammarskjöld's, written by one so deeply immersed in the culture of his age and simultaneously so burdened by the world's most demanding civil office. This fact alone makes our project worthwhile, although it may not be inappropriate to add that confessions *as documents of faith* are primary in relation to theology, since one of theology's main concerns is precisely the interpretation of such documents.

[45] W. H. Auden, Foreword to *Markings*, p. xx.

THE PROFILE OF HAMMARSKJÖLD'S FAITH

Hammarskjöld himself gratefully acknowledged the stimulation and aid he received from others on his way towards faith. But although his frequent use of quotations adds substance to his diary, we are of the opinion that throughout the years Hammarskjöld developed a position of remarkable independence. He did not simply repeat the insights of those who stood as his teachers. Schweitzer, for example, brought him into touch with the critical investigation of the Bible, but Hammarskjöld's reflections concerning the Jesus of the Gospels have their own character, and certainly the faith of *Markings* is not simply a rehearsal of the faith of Albert Schweitzer. Similarly, as we have seen, the medieval mystics were of great importance to Hammarskjöld, especially at the point of language, but Hammarskjöld was not unwilling to depart at significant points from more traditional interpretations of those same mystics. In drawing our picture of the faith of *Markings*, furthermore, we have seen the importance for Hammarskjöld of biblical patterns of speech. At some points, certainly, we may perceive linguistic tensions between the language of mysticism and the language of the Bible; Hammarskjöld himself, however, never saw such tensions.

The profile which we intend to trace, by way of concluding our study, is naturally based upon the analysis we have already presented. We propose, as our method, to point to certain central terms in *Markings*, the first three of which draw our attention to Hammarskjöld's commitment to life: *imitation, sacrifice,* and *responsibility*.

Imitatio was surely one of the key ideas to which the author of *Markings* was exposed in his study of the mystics. Most definitely, however, his notion of imitation was derived from his view of the picture of Jesus presented in the New Testament Gospels. Jesus was the "Brother" to be followed, and the invitation to fellowship with Jesus set forth in the Gospels was accepted by Hammarskjöld as the enduring basis for the true imitation of Christ. In this invitation he found the authentic measure for life.

But *imitatio* is fulfilled by *sacrifice* for the sake of others. It was precisely at this point that Hammarskjöld was engaged by and attached to the Jesus found in the Gospels: in obedience to his apprehension of the will of God, Jesus sacrificed himself for the sake of others, and thus the only proper *imitatio Christi* is similar sacrifice. This is not self-chosen suffering, nor is it, after the manner of Kierkegaard, tribulation rooted in the picture of a God who wishes man to suffer in order to be educated. Sacrifice is self-surrender to others within the framework of one's own vocation. But precisely in this self-surrender is to be found the only authentic self-realization. This self-surrender demands readiness to accept the full consequence of service to others—even the consequence of death.

But beyond any view which might be seen as essentially negative, Hammarskjöld embraced an understanding of sacrifice as the truly creative power in existence. As such a power, it reveals the Christ who not only demands *imitatio* but who also mediates the forgiveness of God's love. Indeed, for Hammarskjöld forgiveness always entailed a sacrifice, and from this position he could view the Jesus who appears in the Gospels as the "Son" in the "Trinity." Yet, even in this context, the word *Son* can be used interchangeably with the word *Brother:* Father, Brother, Spirit.

A commitment to life which strives for realization in imitation and sacrifice provokes an intense feeling of *responsibility*. For Hammarskjöld this responsibility was intensified by the office entrusted to him, the "calling" to which he had been "dedicated." He was required "to give his all" to that which was at once "a feeble human dream" and "the greatest creation of mankind." He was required to serve the world as a whole— and he saw such service of mankind as service to God. Aware of these awesome requirements, he submitted himself to ruthless self-criticism: "Your responsibility is indeed terrifying. If you fail, it is God, thanks to your having betrayed Him, who will fail mankind. You fancy you can be responsible *to* God; can you carry the responsibility *for* God?" (p. 133). Contrary to certain misunderstandings which appeared when *Markings* was first published, Hammarskjöld is not here proposing to step into God's place. Rather, man as an instrument of God's will possesses the power to betray God, thus converting constructive work into a power of destruction. When God's intention is thus thwarted, he has— in Hammarskjöld's sense—failed mankind. A direct translation of the first Swedish words of this passage is eloquent: "How terrifying, *our* responsibility" (italics mine). The English translation does not convey this rare instance in which Hammarskjöld uses the word *our;* here, he is not thinking only of himself.

THE PROFILE OF HAMMARSKJÖLD'S FAITH

Hammarskjöld's commitment ultimately depends on his *commitment to God*. Indeed, there is no feature in *Markings* more striking than that of the union between these two commitments. To be united with God, to be in his hands, means to rest in his stillness, to receive strength and inspiration from him, to be liberated by him and to live in freedom. In his important statement from Whitsunday 1961, as in many earlier passages, Hammarskjöld describes this freedom with the biblical words, "not to look back" and "to take no thought for the morrow." But union with God always means at the same time union with men, and union is to be realized in the service of men. This entire emphasis is accentuated most strikingly in the crucial declaration that, in our era, the road to sanctification necessarily passes through action.

A major question which here arises is the meaning of the word *God* for Hammarskjöld. Here again we must direct our attention to three principal expressions: God as the *creating power*, God as *the One*, God as the *mystery of love*.

Creation is a word of utmost importance in *Markings*. This does not mean that anything is to be found there about creation "in the beginning," or about the relation between creation and science. Hammarskjöld's interest in creation is above all to accentuate that God's creation is perpetual and that in its steady continuation it stands as the very opposite of chaos. At New Year's 1958 he expressed this: "So shall the world be created each morning anew, *forgiven*—in Thee, by Thee" (p. 138). Chaos is evil; to create means to overcome the evil. Hope for the world polluted by evil is based on the fact that God is always creating and that he will not cease to create until his kingdom is realized. Therefore, we ought not to despair: "Thou who has created us free, Who seest all that happens—yet art confident of victory" (p. 92).

From all of this, it is perfectly consistent that Hammarskjöld's decisive question should be: "Do you create? / Or destroy? *That's* / for your ordeal-by-fire to answer" (p. 158). To destroy is to betray God; to create is to serve him—to have a part in the creating work of the God "who does wonders." In such service, Hammarskjöld says, "each of your acts is an act of creation, conscious, because you are a human being with human responsibilities, but governed, nevertheless, by the power beyond human consciousness which has created man" (p. 139).

This view of the continuously creative activity of God, in opposition to chaos and evil, discloses a dramatic outlook in which existence becomes deeply meaningful—something often emphasized in *Markings*. It is the creating God from whom emanates the universal perspective which we have described. God's power is not limited to the sphere of Christendom. There are no limits at all to his creative power. Wherever chaos and evil are forced to cease, wherever destruction is replaced by construction, there God's creative power has been at work.

The description of God as *the One*—or Oneness or Wholeness—is derived from the language of the mystics. The meaning of such expressions Hammarskjöld can give by saying that in God we meet "reality" or "the ultimate reality." At one point he quotes Psalm 51: "But lo, thou requirest truth in the inward parts: and shall make me to understand wisdom secretly." Then, as a kind of comment, he continues: "In 'faith'—an unbroken living contact with all things. 'Before God,' therefore the soul is *in reality"* (p. 147*; italics mine; the English translation says: in truth). This reality is ultimate: "Only when you descend into yourself and encounter the Other, do you then experience goodness as the ultimate reality—united and living—*in* Him and *through* you" (p. 139).

What does this description of God as the One mean for a person's relationship to him? There are, I think, at least three consequences. Two of them appear in the following declaration: "In the faith . . . you are *one* in God, and God is wholly in you, just as, for you, He is wholly in all you meet" (p. 139). To be *one* in God means personal integrity; the opposite is, to be divided: "the chaos you become whenever God's hand does not rest upon your head" (p. 95). To be alienated from the One means anxiety: "The intense blaze of your anxiety reveals to what a great extent you are still fettered, still alienated from the One" (p. 132). Further, to be in the One means to meet God everywhere in existence, and not least in men who are to be served. This is central to *Markings*— important for many reasons, including the fact that it shows that the "vertical" perspective of relationship with God, realized in meditation and prayer, cannot be separated from the "horizontal" perspective in which God meets us in men and in the world. Thus, these two perspectives become one, illustrating—and also illustrated by—Hammarskjöld's affirmation that the road to sanctification, in our era, passes through action. Finally, the view of God as the ultimate reality means that faith in God can be a life in harmony with existence as a whole or, as Hammarskjöld himself expresses it, "a humble and spontaneous response to Life" (p. 147).

Ultimately, the focus in which all of these aspects converge is the *mystery of love*. The creative power of God is the power of love, the quality of which has been primarily revealed in the sacrifice of the cross. Jesus our Brother, therefore, is the core and nucleus of love; he discloses the creative power of sacrifice. The love of God, in spite of all that contradicts it, is "the ultimate reality." To be united with God and in his hand is the gift of love and, at the same time, the exertion of the claim of God on man. Without love, *imitatio* and sacrifice are nothing. The road to sanctification passes through action; but sanctification means to be "in the Light"—"self-effaced so that it may be focused and spread wider" (p. 133*).

The love of God is a mystery. Love, Hammarskjöld says, is a much misused and misinterpreted word which shares the inadequacies of all expressions used in reference to God. Nevertheless, no other word can compete with *love*. Its mystery is not only hidden behind that which faith experiences, but also appears in that very experience—not least in the reception of God's forgiveness.

Hammarskjöld's confessions show how deeply he experienced existence as meaningless, how intensely he felt the loneliness of alienation from existence, and how perspicaciously he viewed the evil powers at work in the world. Through all of this experience, furthermore, Hammarskjöld persisted in ruthless self-criticism. About this experience there is not necessarily anything unique, as the literature of our time so eloquently attests. Yet in *Markings* Hammarskjöld manifests an unshaken faith in God, a faith which provided meaning for his life and for his view of existence as a whole. And against the background of such experience it is no wonder that this faith in the love of God should appear as *mystery* even as it appears as *ultimate reality*.

We have given, in this concluding summary and throughout our entire study, an affirmative answer to the question whether or not Dag Hammarskjöld's faith, as it appears in *Markings,* has a profile of its own. We have endeavored to trace this profile on the basis of those elements which seem to pervade his thoughts and, certainly, not on the basis of isolated passages in the book. *Markings* can profitably be seen as though it were a musical composition. We are accustomed in listening to music to hearing well-known themes treated in novel ways and with unexpected connections. This is the case, for example, with contemporary settings of the Mass in which we can distinguish both the Gregorian tradition of chant and melodies unique to our own era. This combination of old and modern tonalities, when successfully carried out, serves to accentuate the originality and beauty of each. So it is with *Markings*. Here we find the traditional themes of faith, sometimes appearing in the simplicity of prayer; and here we find sophisticated insights which build upon impressive learning and historical judgment and, in addition, upon the burdens of Hammarskjöld's singular vocation. In *Markings* we read nothing of the issues and dilemmas which make the United Nations a place of such great significance, but the sound of the world's storms is clearly to be heard in, with, and under the meditations. Like good, new music which pays heed to tradition, the combination of these ingredients gives to *Markings* a profile of its own.

Let us underscore the point that our analysis has not been aimed at leading Hammarskjöld into some confessional or theological fold—such a procedure would have been out of place, dishonest, and irrelevant. We can correctly surmise that the author of *Markings* would have been content to describe himself as a "disciple of the Gospels." Yet this would not necessarily involve him in a denial of his heritage—national, intellectual, or spiritual. He was, in fact, deeply rooted in the fullness of that heritage, as he so eloquently maintained in his address, "On the Upsala Tradition," delivered in 1956 at America's Upsala College in East Orange, New Jersey,[46] and as he confessed in the following passage from *Markings*. The entry was written at a time when he was burdened by the loneliness of his office; the opening phrase is from St. John Perse. " 'The flutes of exile.' Forever among strangers to all that has shaped your life —*alone*. Forever thirsting for the living waters—but not even free to seek them, a *prisoner*" (p. 132).

[46] Dag Hammarskjöld, "On the Upsala Tradition," in *Servant of Peace* (see n. 1 above), p. 118.

The fact that something from the church was included in Hammarskjöld's spiritual heritage can be denied only if that church is seen as nothing but a "rigid Lutheran orthodoxy"—and, of course, that was not the case. Some part of the influence of the Church of Sweden on Hammarskjöld may have passed through secret channels; nevertheless that influence persisted, as we have shown in the comparisons made in this chapter. But, what is more, Hammarskjöld openly rendered account of his debt to his tradition. It is not pure chance that he often quotes the Swedish hymnal. The quotation from E. G. Geijer at the beginning of 1955 (p. 103)[47] could—in its original form and meaning, not in the meaningless English rendering of *Markings*—very well act as a motto for his whole diary. Another part of Hammarskjöld's debt to his tradition is the ecumenical outlook championed originally by Archbishop Söderblom and acknowledged in his speech to the Assembly of the World Council of Churches in 1954.

I need not say that for Hammarskjöld there was no contradiction between "national" and "international." Of course he opposed all nationalistic tendencies, but he saw "national" and "international" together. He often emphasized his conviction that one must first of all come to terms with his own culture if he is to understand any other culture or develop a truly international understanding. And this same conviction he applied to his understanding of the religions of the world.

My attempt to analyze the constitution of Hammarskjöld's "white book" has come to a close. We have seen a shy man open his heart. At the end of 1956 he discusses the possibility that the diary might be published. He talks of its entries as "signposts" for his own use and then continues: "But your life has changed, and now you reckon with possible readers, even, perhaps, hope for them. Still, perhaps it may be of interest to somebody to learn about a path about which the traveler who was committed to it did not wish to speak while he was alive" (p. 125). *Markings* has found many readers in many countries, and we are grateful that publication took place. My analysis has, I hope, shown something of the book's richness. *Markings* is for every kind of reader—for the one

---

[47] See p. 84 above.

unfamiliar with Christian faith, for the one struggling to find a faith, and for the one who has already offered his commitment.

The final word will be left to Hammarskjöld himself. Even though the question of death seems always to have been close to him, he seldom combined it with the thought of eternity. It is clear, though, that eternity for him, as in the Gospel of John, is to be experienced in the midst of this life—presently, in God's union with the soul—as the overcoming of death. We have pointed to two places in *Markings* (pp. 84, 105) where Hammarskjöld writes in this vein; let us now point to a third. Here he uses familiar and important symbols, the storm and the sail. Once before, he wrote about the wind and a sail: " 'The *Wind* bloweth where it listeth'. . . . Like wind— In it, with it, *of* it. Of it just like a sail, so light and strong that, even when it is bent flat, it gathers all the power of the wind without hampering its course" (p. 112). Now the wind has become a storm, a "sun storm." He writes on June 11, 1961, just three months before his death, in a time when the burden of office and life is heavy. We read his poem as a vignette of farewell (p. 173):

> Summoned
> To carry it,
> Alone
> To assay it,
> Chosen
> To suffer it,
> And free
> To deny it,
> I saw
> For one moment
> The sail
> In the sun storm,
> Far off
> On a wave crest,
> Alone,
> Bearing from land.
>
> For one moment
> I saw.